BILLY BISHOP GOES TO WAR

BILLY BISHOP GOES TO WAR

Second Edition

JOHN MACLACHLAN GRAY
WITH ERIC PETERSON

Talonbooks

Copyright © 1981, 2012 Colonial Repertory Theatre Company Ltd.

Talonbooks
278 East First Avenue, Vancouver, British Columbia, Canada V5T 1A6
talonbooks.com

Typeset in Frutiger Serif.
Printed and bound in Canada on 100% post-consumer recycled paper.
Typeset & cover design by Typesmith. Cover illustration by Alan Hindle.

Second printing, second edition: 2018

The publisher gratefully acknowledges the financial support of the Canada Council for the Arts, the Government of Canada through the Canada Book Fund, and the Province of British Columbia through the British Columbia Arts Council and the Book Publishing Tax Credit for our publishing activities.

Grateful acknowledgement is made to the photographers listed for permission to reprint previously published work. Every effort has been made to contact copyright holders; in the event of an inadvertent omission or error, please notify the publisher.

Library and Archives Canada Cataloguing in Publication

Gray, John, 1946–

    Billy Bishop goes to war / John MacLachlan Gray with Eric Peterson. — 2nd ed.

Issued also in electronic format.
ISBN 978-0-88922-689-0

    1. Bishop, William A., 1894–1956—Drama. 2. World War, 1914–1918—Aerial operations, British—Drama. I. Peterson, Eric, 1946– II. Title.

PS8563.R411B5 2012   C812'.54   C2012-904694-9

For William Avery Bishop, whoever he was

*Remember that what you are told is really threefold:
shaped by the teller, reshaped by the listener,
concealed from both by the dead man of the tale.*

— VLADIMIR NABOKOV

INTRODUCTION

Like all major developments in the thirty-four-year-and-counting evolution of the Canadian musical play *Billy Bishop Goes to War*, the opportunity came from out of the blue, and under singular circumstances.

Albert Schultz, artistic director of Soulpepper Theatre, arguably Toronto's premier theatre company, had a crisis on his hands: three days before the 2009 season was to be announced (website going up, press releases emailed, pamphlets sent to the printers, technicians signed, buckets of money spent), an actor had abruptly cancelled his contract – not just any actor, but the star of a one-man show with piano accompaniment.

Such emergencies occur in any undertaking that involves multiple human components, and the theatre is no exception. Planning a season is an enterprise of enormous complexity, in which a sort of ecological balance must be achieved among dozens of variables – personal, technical, financial, cosmetic; losing one show doesn't just create a hole in the season, it throws the whole ecology out of whack, like what happens to the balance of nature when a particular species goes extinct.

If Schultz failed to find a replacement with a roughly similar cast, technical requirements, and cost, he would have to redesign his entire lineup, and there wasn't time for that. It was a theatrical emergency analogous to the plot reversal in the musical *42nd Street*, in which the lead literally breaks a leg, just before opening night.

"Could you and Eric possibly do *Billy Bishop*?" came the inquiry from Schultz. "Please say yes."

(I didn't know you could hear a man sweat over the phone.)

Eric was hesitant and so was I – if only because, over the years since we'd last performed the play, we had detected no upsurge of public demand for these two superannuated hoofers to perform their tale yet again. Meanwhile, our child had left the house, found a paying job, and was sending money home. For decades, the play had served as a reliable, popular, well-reviewed, cheap addition to a season; accordingly, actors all over North America had kept the play in their back pockets as their "party piece" – which sounds cynical but isn't really. Every actor who plays the role ends up feeling that in some way he is Billy Bishop, and when called upon can get into the part like a bespoke suit, made just for him.

Bishop is a terrific part for an actor, but there is nothing magical about how it got that way. Never in the history of theatre has a script received more audience-inspired revisions by its creators; hundreds of performances in North America and Great Britain, and never once did we stop tinkering with the thing.

Director Mike Nichols described how it is relatively easy to edit the parts of a performance that bore the audience witless; the big challenge comes when you start dealing with moments – a gesture, a line, a word or two – during which the audience becomes *almost* bored. Such lapses accrue, and their cumulative effect is to bring on a sort of metal fatigue, weakening the entire experience.

If you have the stomach to observe and admit to these weak moments, the best and most effective place from which to do this is while performing onstage, where you can sense that slight withdrawal of collective attention, a variance in intensity that says you haven't quite nailed the moment yet. If it happens once or twice, you can blame it on the vagaries of live performance, the stupidity of the audience, the acoustics, the seating, the weather; but when you feel that flat spot over several performances, with audiences in different cities, eventually you have nothing to blame but your script. And it is always truly amazing how the elimination of an extraneous word or phrase, a few seconds really, can suddenly make a scene feel five minutes shorter.

But in 2009, after more than thirty years, the play was unlikely to benefit from any more tinkering.

As well, in the practical terms of our careers in showbiz, neither Eric nor I really needed another go at it. Throughout the 1980s and '90s we had been practising our trades with varying degrees of success – Eric played numerous roles onstage and TV, while I churned out novels, reviews, TV and radio punditry, nonfiction books, newspaper columns, satirical videos, screenplays, and musicals for the stage. There was no reason to think that performing *Billy Bishop Goes to War* yet again would do us any further good; and, as Lady St. Helier would put it, by taking the play on at this late date we could make a real "balls-up" of it. After all, at sixty-two we were well into life's Act III, and nobody wants to exit with a whimper.

And another thing: if we accepted, unless I proposed to inhabit Eric's Toronto basement like a rodent sleeping on a futon, I would be spending major time in that most dreaded of accommodations, the Furnished Suite: the IKEA coffee table. The inexplicable prints on the wall. The instructions on the fridge.

On the other hand, our calendars had become relatively clear up to the end of the twenty-first century. Moreover, this was an opportunity for two old comrades (known privately as the Hardly Boys) to reconnect, by collaborating on the project that had brought us together in the first place.

≈

As friends and colleagues, Eric and I go way back. Our intermittent association began around 1970, when the University of British Columbia theatre department had become a magnet for young actors and directors who either couldn't get into the National Theatre School of Canada, or didn't want to – students who didn't see why an acting program spent so much time teaching people to imitate English accents, in an era when more relevant-seeming models (if also foreign) had presented themselves: Grotowski's Poor Theatre; the Performance Group; the Living Theatre; the Open Theatre – companies that functioned more like rock bands than like English stock and rep companies.

Some of this generation of UBC theatre students later formed just such a group (it became known as Tamahnous, a Chilcotin word for sorcery); our first show was a version of *Dracula Two*, a piece first assembled by the Stables Theatre Company in Manchester (the actor who played Lucy came from Manchester), with Eric eating flies as the central character, Renfield.

Rehearsing *Dracula Two* as actor and director, we found ourselves collaborating in interesting ways, working from outside and inside the machine, entertaining extreme notions, communicating by making each other laugh.

Tom Stoppard once described laughter as "the sound of comprehension," but it's more than that, it's an admission of fact. Laughter is like throwing up or having an epileptic fit – you can't deny you did it. Some sort of truth is out in the open. And at some point during our rehearsals and performances, Eric and I made a discovery that became a pact: if we both laughed, then it was worth doing. (Peterson will never let go of the time I was cutting his hair and I stumbled, nearly piercing his jugular. Forty-two years, and he still brings that up.)

Admittedly, our early work was highly derivative, but it wasn't easy to find Canadian models back then, especially in Vancouver, where they didn't exist. Factory Theatre in Toronto, also founded in 1970, was the only company in the country devoted to original Canadian work. The rest relied on classics and imported hits, with the odd Canadian remount thrown in, only if necessary.

Unfortunately, Canadian plays at that time enjoyed the same reputation as Canadian music, Canadian TV, Canadian movies, and Canadian history for that matter: as essentially uninteresting, as though the ability to entertain were missing from the Canadian gene pool. (Odd how so many different races and cultures with the same passport could have been lumped together in a single boring adjective.)

But original, authentic work does not happen because somebody wants to be original and authentic. It sneaks in when you're just trying to figure how to interest an audience. Someone gets an idea that might "work," and only afterward does anyone mention that they haven't seen it done before. In those days, original work was happening; it was just that nobody thought about it as such.

Sometime in 1973 Eric emigrated to Toronto, where there were more than two professional theatre companies, and therefore a chance in hell of getting paid to work. I followed two years later, leaving behind a disintegrated marriage and a short career in haberdashery. By then, Eric was working with Theatre Passe Muraille on a series of plays having to do with something that until then most of us had never thought existed – Canadian heroes.

I watched in astonishment as the company performed Rick Salutin's *1837: The Farmers' Revolt* in a livestock auction barn (I'm not kidding), before an audience of bean and corn farmers and their families. It was the first time I had heard a Canadian accent spoken onstage. It was also the first time I had watched actors base their characters on people they had actually met in their real lives, and not on other actors they admired. The play even contained Canadian violence – the first I'd ever heard about. As our standard school texts had represented it, with the exception of the battle on the Plains of Abraham between the French and the English in which both leaders got killed (constituting a kind of salubrious moral lesson on the pointlessness of war), everything was smooth sailing when it came to Canadian history – really nothing more than a series of business deals.

≈

So here we were, much older, and only too aware of Soulpepper's reputation as a place for serious, A-list talent. If we turned down their offer, was that tantamount to admitting we weren't really in their league, that our work had been very good – for its time?

On the positive side, the production would force me to go back to the piano. It had been years since I had played the thing with any concentration; I had neglected the instrument shamefully, never enjoying practice unless it was for an immediate purpose. But eventually the guilt always piled up, and I would slouch back to the musical theatre like the prodigal son.

Eric and I debated the issues I just covered at such length (for about ten minutes) and then decided to assume a what-the-hell attitude; that we would say yes first and ask questions later.

And oh my, a few months later when we got together and put our minds to it, we had plenty of questions to ponder – the most immediate and difficult being how to make sense (dramatically, thematically, theatrically, and in every other way) of the radical recasting of the principal role, now to be played by a sixty-two-year-old man. Makeup and Botox were not the answer. Humiliating reviews with nightmarish headlines sprang to mind: "Billy Bishop Totters to War"; "Billy Bishop Goes to Bed." (Oddly enough, the latter description turned out to be not far from the reality.)

Billy Bishop Goes to War has always been a toss-up between documentary fact (stuff we found out) and narrative structure (stuff we made up), a sort of juggling act: you keep certain facts, drop others, and draw lines between what you have left to make a story that might as well have been fiction. Though the facts of the story may match the historical record, the staged *Billy Bishop* and the "real" William Avery Bishop resemble one another about the way Burt Lancaster in the film *Gunfight at the O.K. Corral* resembled the "real" Wyatt Earp.

Myth-making is a reductive process. What makes a work seem emblematic and interesting, what transforms real, live people into metaphors, is partly what you write about them, but mostly what you leave out. In this age of reality TV, many people have trouble understanding how metaphors work: how a documentary fiction can reveal more truth in the tale than a factually all-inclusive account.

Hence our persistent indifference, through the many versions of the play over the years, to the unedifying controversies about just how many Germans Bishop killed or didn't kill. (I read a contemporary comment to the effect that, had the official count of enemy casualties been accurate on both sides, no planes would have been left in the air.) To us, what mattered about Billy Bishop wasn't his scorecard, but his experience of being a soldier, a survivor, and a "hero" – a word that offers a virtual litmus test of meanings, depending on what you're selling.

At the same time, Billy Bishop did exist in real life, with children and grandchildren and a legacy that continues to this day, so we weren't about to make things up about him. Everything in the play had to have really happened.

The second thing that became paramount for our geriatric rewrite was something we had already learned from watching other people perform the play over the years: that more than anything else, the storyteller defines the story.

When the Afro-American actor Ben Halley Jr. played Bishop in the mid-1980s (you can watch him on YouTube), it became another show entirely. When Lady St. Helier sings, "Colonials ... / I'm very tired of your whining / And your infantile maligning, / Your own weakness simply won't be whined away," the word "colonials" came across to Halley's Boston audience not as "Canadian" but as "black." On the other hand, performed by a twenty-eight-year-old Ryan Beil in Vancouver and Saskatoon, the play took on an additional layer of pathos – a constant visual reminder that handsome young men of precisely his age were blown to pieces by the tens of thousands. (An especially poignant thought at a time when Canadian soldiers were being killed and mutilated in Afghanistan.)

In the case of our new Soulpepper production, performed January 22 to February 27, 2010, the storyteller would have to be an actor of sixty-two portraying Billy Bishop, who died in Florida, essentially of old age, at the age of, well, sixty-two. Anything beyond that initial premise would have to come out in rehearsal.

~

One of the nicest things about producing a play is that you're not alone. Enter Ted Dykstra, our director, who is also a performer, playwright, and musician – a combination I have always liked in a man.

Ted was not so foolish as to think he would get anywhere with a Director's Concept (for us it was a bit late in the day for that), but he did come in with a Big Idea just the same: that we might wed the fact of our own age and Bishop's age with the fact that we had been performing the play over a long period of time, a confluence between the play and the circumstances of its production that came together through the process of remembering: what it means to look back over the years; the sense of wonder you experience, looking back. As Bishop says in the play, "And all in all I'd have to say … It was a hell of a time."

Inspired by the last spoken line of the play, Ted steered that underlying idea to a place where it's hard for the audience to know for certain who is saying it – Billy Bishop, Eric Peterson, or the two of them together. We would never have dared do that without Ted. We would never have had the nerve. How Canadian of us: just who did we think we were?

Between them, Dykstra and Camilla Koo, the designer, contrived a set that consisted mostly of trunks, stamped with the names of the various theatres we had played over the years. Those trunks were put to a remarkable number of purposes – as chairs, as desks, as the R.E.7 airplane, and as rubble on the battlefield. On the walls surrounding the audience were photographs and other memorabilia. When we made our entrance, we did so from the back of the audience, then stepped on the stage and took a bow, as ourselves.

This meta-layer joining the performers to the character pro-vided a framework for the physical production that entirely eliminated the fourth wall. For not one second did the audience find it necessary to imagine that this was, in fact, Billy Bishop speaking to them. Everybody understood that this was Eric Peter-son, with John Gray at the piano, "acting out" our tale.

Sounds awfully simple, doesn't it? It's a bit like minimalist painting – it looks simple once it's done, but good luck getting there.

With no illusions, no disbelief to suspend, the audience was ready for anything. People felt no disruption, for example, when a woman in the front row suffered a bout of coughing, and Eric / Billy gave her a glass of water. Nor was the show ruined when a troupe of seniors with walkers inched down the aisle twenty minutes late; Eric / Billy simply announced an interlude, during which I played whatever tune came to mind and he did a little dance. Who was dancing right then – Peterson or Bishop?

That's live theatre for you: a welcome contrast to the all-pervasive electronic media, in which everything has already happened; in which the audience is watching a *fait accompli* that, no matter how they react, will be exactly the same performance tomorrow night and the night after that, and will last forever, like Styrofoam.

If there is any future for live performance as an art form, surely it lies in the fact that, as with anything that matters in life, if you miss it, you missed it. The experience is not online. It is not on demand.

(Despite my snipes at film and TV, the Soulpepper production did actually become an excellent movie, one that uses the stage play to create something quite different – an opera going on inside a man's head. It was directed by Barbara Willis Sweete, produced by Strada Films, and broadcast on CBC Television in 2010.)

The new concept fit the script in ways that surprised me; for example, take the fact that Bishop performed in pyjamas and dressing gown: suddenly we became aware of the number of times that Bishop finds himself wearing pyjamas – whether in hospital, or called on the carpet by Lady St. Helier, or about to attack the enemy at dawn: "and why didn't I change out of my pyjamas? That's going to be great if I'm taken prisoner, real dignified, spend the rest of the war in my bloody pyjamas!"

Meanwhile for the Piano Player, it's not every day you get to play music you not only wrote but have played and sung so often that it's practically in your genetic code – the way Bob Dylan knows "Blowin' in the Wind" so well that he can give it a different nuance every time he plays it. For a performer, this leads to the rare experience of being entirely in the present tense, freed of the raven on one's shoulder crying, not "Nevermore," but "Naw"!

When we sang "Friends ain't s'posed to die 'til they're old," I would remember Tommy Smith, our American stage manager, who died of AIDS in 1983; and Larry Lillo, a UBC colleague who directed nearly every show I wrote until he died in 1993; not to mention 160 or so Canadian youngsters killed in Afghanistan, so far. When audiences teared up at that song, so did the piano player. As Eric puts it, "Before, when Bishop sang about survival I took it as a romantic thing to do with the war. But now it's become a metaphor for life. The price of survival is that you experience the death of your friends."

Of course, the difference between war and "normal life" is that war is faster and more compressed. A young man barely out of his teens experiences in six months what the rest of us, if we're lucky and wise, process and understand by the time we're collecting our pensions. But in both cases, young or old, survival takes courage.

For all the praise it has received, *Billy Bishop Goes to War* is, at bottom, a piece of make-believe. We are humbled and abashed whenever we meet men and women who experienced the real thing.

All in all, I think I learned more from the writing and performance of the 2009 version of *Billy Bishop* than all its predecessors combined: that, as Bishop puts it, "None of us are in control of these things, are we?" And that big ideas are preferable to little ones. And that friendship is stronger than death.

≈

The script that follows is necessarily two scripts, depending on the age of the actor as storyteller. Differences in the two versions appear as explanatory stage directions. The dialogue is identical throughout, except for the ending: in one case, the younger Bishop flashes forward to World War II, as he rallies the troops while in his mid-forties; in the other, the elder Bishop writes a last letter to Margaret at age sixty-two.

But really, it is the same play it always was – just as Peterson and Gray are the same people we were at thirty-two. The difference is in the telling.

— JOHN MACLACHLAN GRAY

July 2012

John MacLachlan Gray at age thirty-two.
Photo by John Vossos

A PHOTOGRAPHIC HISTORY

Captain W.A. Bishop, V.C., Royal Flying Corps (1917).
Photo by William Rider-Rider, LAC PA-001654

Eric Peterson as flying ace Bishop in Tamahnous /
Vancouver East Cultural Centre production (1978).
Photo by Glen Erikson

Punch caricature published during the London production at the
Comedy Theatre (1981)

(left)
Eric Peterson dons flying helmet and goggles in New York production (1980)

Eric Peterson in still from National Film Board of Canada documentary
The Kid Who Couldn't Miss (1983)

John MacLachlan Gray with Hans-Peter Korff as Bishop in West German Broadcasting (WDR) TV film *Billy Bishop steigt aus* (1984), German translation by Hans Magnus Enzensberger

The one time Eric Peterson actually flew, thanks to the ingenuity of designer Sue Lepage and the special-effects company Walter Klassen FX, who designed a carbon-fibre rig lined with sheepskin that enabled Eric to perform manoeuvres in mid-air during the Canadian Stage production (1998). Photo by David Cooper

Eric Peterson in Soulpepper Production (2010).
Photo by Cylla von Tiedemann

John MacLachlan Gray and Eric Peterson in Strada Films
Billy Bishop Goes to War (2010).
Photo by Ben Mark Holzberg

BILLY BISHOP GOES TO WAR

PRODUCTION HISTORY

Billy Bishop Goes to War opened on November 3, 1978,
at the Vancouver East Cultural Centre, produced by the
Vancouver East Cultural Centre in association
with Tamahnous Theatre.

CAST LIST

BILLY BISHOP: Eric Peterson
NARRATOR / PIANO PLAYER: John MacLachlan Gray

Directed by John MacLachlan Gray
Set and Lighting Design by Paul Williams
Music and Lyrics by John MacLachlan Gray

CHARACTERS

NARRATOR / PIANO PLAYER

BILLY BISHOP, *who also plays*

    DRILL SERGEANT

    AN UPPERCLASSMAN

    ADJUTANT PERRAULT

    AN AIRMAN

    SIR HUGH CECIL

    LADY ST. HELIER

    CEDRIC, *her butler*

    A DOCTOR

    OFFICER ONE

    OFFICER TWO

    GENERAL JOHN HIGGINS, *Brigade Commander*

    A TOMMY

    THE LOVELY HÉLÈNE

    ALBERT BALL

    WALTER BOURNE, *Bishop's mechanic*

    A GERMAN

    GENERAL HUGH M. TRENCHARD

    AN ADJUTANT

    SECOND OFFICER

    KING GEORGE V

ACT ONE

*Lights up on BILLY BISHOP and the PIANO
PLAYER, on a stage containing memorabilia,
much of it from the Great War. The setting could
be an officer's mess, a Legion bar, a cluttered
room in Bishop's house, or the attic of a veteran's
hospital. BISHOP sits in a vintage chair. The
PIANO PLAYER – he could be an old friend or a
memory – sits at the piano and sings.*

BISHOP & PIANO PLAYER: (*singing*)
*We were off to fight the Hun,
We would shoot him with a gun.
Our medals would shine
Like a sabre in the sun.
We were off to fight the Hun
And it looked like lots of fun,
Somehow it didn't seem like war
At all, at all, at all.
Somehow it didn't seem like war at all.*

*BISHOP speaks both to the audience and to the
PIANO PLAYER, who continues to accompany
him with a nostalgic chord sequence – amused or
poignant, depending on the actor's age.*

BISHOP:

I think when you haven't been in a war for a while ...
you've got to take what you can get. I mean, Canada?
1914? They must have been pretty desperate. Take me, for
instance. Twenty years old, a convicted liar and cheat – I
mean, I'm on record as the worst student RMC – Royal
Military College in Kingston, Ontario – I'm on record as the
worst student they ever had. I join up, they made me an
officer! A lieutenant in the Mississauga Horse. All I can say
is, they must have been scraping the bottom of the barrel.

BISHOP & PIANO PLAYER: (*singing*)
> *We were off to fight the Hun,*
> *Though hardly anyone*
> *Had ever read about a battle,*
> *Much less seen a Lewis gun.*
> *We were off to fight the Hun*
> *And it looked like lots of fun,*
> *Somehow it didn't seem like war*
> *At all, at all, at all.*
> *Somehow it didn't seem like war at all.*

BISHOP:

Yeah, it looked like it was going to be a great war. I mean, all
my friends were very keen to join up – they were. Not me.
Royal Military College was enough for me. Now the reason I
went to RMC was ... (*tries to remember*)

PIANO PLAYER:

Well, you could ride a horse.

BISHOP:

I could ride a horse. And I was a good shot. I mean, I am a really good shot. I've got these tremendous eyes, you see. And Royal Military College had an entrance exam – which was good because my previous scholastic record wasn't that hot. In fact, when I told my principal that indeed I was going to RMC, he said, "Bishop, you don't have the brains." But I studied real hard, sat for the exams, and got in.

> *The PIANO PLAYER beats a military snare-drum pattern on his knees. BISHOP becomes a DRILL SERGEANT.*

DRILL SERGEANT:

Recruits! Recruits will march at all times, they will not loiter, they will not window-shop. Recruits! Recruits will run at all times through the parade square. Recruits! Recruits will be soundly trounced every Friday night, whether they deserve it or not! (*as himself*) I mean those guys were nuts! They were going to make leaders out of us – the theory being that before you could lead, you had to learn to obey. So because of this we were all assigned to an upperclassman as a kind of, well, slave. And I got assigned to this real sadistic SOB, this guy named Vivian Bishop – that's right, it's the same surname as me; and because of this, I had to tuck him in at night, kiss him on the forehead, and say, "Goodnight, sir!"

PIANO PLAYER:

Daddy. Goodnight, Daddy.

BISHOP:

(*mortified*) Goodnight, Daddy. I mean, it was pretty hard to take some of this stuff seriously. One of my punishments: I'm s'posed to clean out this old Martello tower by the edge of the lake. I mean, it's filthy, hasn't been cleaned in years. Now I do a real great job. I clean it up really well. This upperclassman comes along to inspect it.

BISHOP becomes both the UPPERCLASSMAN and himself.

UPPERCLASSMAN:

What's this in the corner, Bishop?

BISHOP:

That? (*looks carefully*) That's a spider, sir.

UPPERCLASSMAN:

That's right, Bishop. That's a spider. Now you had orders to clean this place up. You haven't done it. Now you get down on your hands and knees and you eat that spider.

BISHOP:

(*to the audience*) I had to eat a spider, in front of all my classmates. You ever had to eat a spider? In public? I doubt it. Nuts! Now whenever I'm not happy, whenever I'm not having a really good time, I do one of three things: I get sick, I get injured, or I get in an awful lot of trouble. My third year at RMC, I got into a lot of trouble. This friend of mine, Townsend? One night we got a bottle of gin and we stole a canoe. Well, we'd arranged to meet these girls out on ...: what was it?

PIANO PLAYER:

Cedar Island. Dead Man's Bay.

BISHOP:

Cedar Island out on Dead Man's Bay. Of course, the canoe
tips over. Now it's early spring, it's really cold. We get
back to shore somehow, and we're just like this (*shivering
violently*), and Townsend says, "Bish, Bish, I've got to go to
the infirmary, I think I've got pneumonia." And I say to him,
"Well, whatever you do, you silly bugger, put on some dry
clothes." Because we couldn't let on what we were doing – I
mean, we're absent without leave, in possession of alcohol,
and we stole a canoe. What I didn't know was, the officer
on duty witnessed this whole thing. Townsend goes to the
infirmary, he's confronted with these charges, he admits
everything. I didn't know that. I'm rudely awakened out of
my sleep and hauled before old Adjutant Perrault.

> *At attention, he addresses ADJUTANT PERRAULT,
> who is French-Canadian.*

Sir? I've been in my bed all night, sir. I really don't know
what you're talking about, sir –

PERRAULT:

Come on, come on now, Bishop. We have the testimony
of the officer on duty. We also have the confession of your
accomplice implicating you fully in this. Now what is your
story, Bishop?

BISHOP:

(*to the audience*) Well, I figure I'm in too deep to change my story. (*to PERRAULT*) Sir, I still maintain –

PERRAULT:

Bishop! I'm going to say the worst thing I can say to a gentleman cadet: you are a liar, Bishop!

The PIANO PLAYER winces and looks away.
BISHOP is momentarily sobered by the memory.

BISHOP:

I got twenty-eight days restricted leave for that. It's like house arrest. Then they caught me cheating on my final exams – well, I handed in the crib notes with the exam paper! And that's when they called me the worst student RMC ever had. They weren't going to tell me what my punishment was until the next fall, so I could stew about it all summer, but I knew what it was going to be. Expulsion. With full honours. But then the war broke out and I enlisted and was made an officer – I mean, for me, it was the lesser of two evils. But everyone else was very keen on the whole thing. They were!

BISHOP & PIANO PLAYER: (*singing*)
We were off to fight the Hun,
Though hardly anyone
Had ever seen a Hun,
Wouldn't know one if we saw one.
We were off to fight the Hun
And it looked like lots of fun,

Somehow it didn't seem like war
At all, at all, at all.
Somehow it didn't seem like war at all.

> *More military rhythm from the PIANO PLAYER.*

BISHOP:

October 1st, 1914! The First Contingent of the Canadian Expeditionary Force left for England! I wasn't with them. I was in the hospital. Thinking of Margaret.

> *The PIANO PLAYER plays the "Dearest Margaret" theme while BISHOP narrates a letter to an old photograph.*

Dear ... Dearest Margaret. I am in the hospital with pneumonia. I also have an allergy. The doctors don't know what I am allergic to. Maybe it's horses. Maybe it's the army. The hospital is nice, so am in good spirits. Thinking of you constantly, I remain ...

> *Again the PIANO PLAYER slaps out a military rhythm on his knees.*

March 1915! The Second, Third, Fourth, Fifth, and Sixth Contingents of the Canadian Expeditionary Force left for England! I wasn't with them either. I was back in the hospital. Thinking of Margaret.

> *Another letter, spoken to the "Dearest Margaret" musical theme.*

Dearest Margaret. Please excuse my writing, as I have a badly sprained wrist. Yesterday my horse reared up and fell over backward on me. It was awful, I could have been killed. My head was completely buried in the mud. My nose is of course broken and quite swollen, I can't see out of one eye, I have two broken ribs, and am pretty badly bruised, but the doctor figures I'll be up and around by Monday. The hospital is nice, so am in fine spirits. Thinking of you constantly, I remain ...

The PIANO PLAYER once again slaps out a military rhythm on his knees.

July 1915! The Seventh Contingent of the Canadian Expeditionary Force left for England! And I was with them!

The PIANO PLAYER plays an anticipatory bass roll.

Now this was aboard a cattle boat, called the *Caledonia*, in Montreal. There was this big crowd came down to the pier to see us off, I mean, hundreds and hundreds of people, and for a while there, I felt like the whole thing was worth doing. I mean, it's pretty impressive when you look out there and you see hundreds and hundreds of people waving – at you. When you're from a small town, the numbers get to you. And you're looking out at them, and they're looking at you, and you think, "Boy, I must be doing something right!"

The PIANO PLAYER breaks into "God Save the King."

And they play "God Save the King," and everybody is crying and waving and cheering, and the boat pulls out, and they start to yell like you never heard anybody yell before – I mean, you feel good, you really do! And we're all praying, "Please, God, don't let the fighting be over before I can take part in it!" (*He gets carried away.*) "On the edge of destiny, you must test your strength!" (*pause, as he comes to his senses*) What the hell am I talking about?

> The PIANO PLAYER plays a monotonous bass
> pattern suggesting the roll of a ship.

The good ship *Caledonia* quickly changed its name to the good ship *Vomit*. It was never meant to hold people. Even the horses didn't like it. Up. Down. Up. Down. And they're siphoning brandy down our throats to keep us from puking our guts up on deck. It was a big joke. Whenever someone would puke, which was every minute or so, everyone would point and laugh like it was the funniest thing you ever saw. I mean, puke swishing around the deck two inches deep, har, har, har!

> Ship's bells on piano suggest a calm sea.

You couldn't sleep, even when it was calm, because every time you closed your eyes, you had this nightmare about torpedoes. (*demonstrates a torpedo to ominous accompaniment*) Every time I closed my eyes I could see this torpedo coming through the water, through the hull of the ship, and ... BOOM!

*The PIANO PLAYER plays a crash of clustered
bass notes.*

And we were torpedoed just off the coast of Ireland. I
was scared shitless. All you could do was stand at the rail
and watch the other ships get hit and go down. Bodies ...
floating around like driftwood in the water. But we made
it through. The good ship *Caledonia*, latrine of the Atlantic,
finally made it through to Portsmouth, full of dead horses
and sick Canadians. When we got off, they thought we were
a boatload of Balkan refugees.

BISHOP & PIANO PLAYER: (*singing*)
> *We were off to fight the Hun,*
> *We would shoot him with a gun.*
> *Our medals would shine*
> *Like a sabre in the sun.*
> *We were off to fight the Hun*
> *And it looked like lots of fun,*
> *Somehow it didn't seem like war*
> *At all, at all, at all.*
> *Somehow it didn't seem like war at all.*

BISHOP:
> A few days later, we marched into Shorncliffe Military
> Camp, right on the Channel. On a clear night you could see
> the artillery flashes from France.

> *Distant explosions on piano.*

> I took it as a sign of better things to come. It wasn't.

*BISHOP narrates another letter to the "Dearest
Margaret" theme.*

Dearest Margaret. Shorncliffe Military Camp is the worst
yet. The wind brings two kinds of weather – either it rains
or it doesn't. When it rains, you've got mud like I've never
seen before. Your horse gets stuck in a foot and a half of
mud, you get off – and you're knee deep. The rain falls in
sheets; you're never, ever dry. Then the rain stops and the
ground dries out – what a relief, you say. But then the wind
gets the dust going and you've got dust storms for days.
The sand is like needles hitting you: a lot of the men are
bleeding from the eyes. I don't know which is worse – going
blind or going crazy. The sand gets into your food, your
clothes, your tent, your … body orifices. A lot of the guys
have something called desert madness, which is really
serious. As I write this letter, the sand is drifting across the
page. Thinking of you constantly, I remain …

*The PIANO PLAYER brings "Dearest Margaret"
theme to a melancholy end while BISHOP ruefully
ponders his fate.*

Being buried alive in the mud. I was seriously considering
this prospect one day, when a funny thing happened.
(*demonstrating*) You see, I got my horse stuck in the middle
of the parade ground. The horse is up to its fetlocks, I'm up
to my knees, mud, sweat, and horseshit from head to toe …

*The PIANO PLAYER plays an ethereal "flying"
theme, reminiscent of Ravel or Debussy.*

Then suddenly, out of the clouds comes this little single-seater scout, this little fighter plane. It circles a couple of times – I guess the pilot had lost his way and was coming down to ask for directions. He does this turn, then lands on an open space, like a dragonfly on a rock. The pilot jumps out – he's in this long sheepskin coat, helmet, goggles ... Warm and dry. He gets his directions, then jumps back into the machine and up in the air, with the mist blowing off him. All by himself. No superior officer. No horse. No sand, no mud – what a beautiful picture. I don't know how long I stood there watching, until he was long gone. Out of sight.

*The music ends. BISHOP abruptly breaks
the mood.*

I mean, this war was going on a lot longer than anyone expected. A lot more people were getting killed than anyone expected, too. Now I sure as hell wasn't going to spend the rest of the war in the mud. And I wasn't going to die in the mud!

*The PIANO PLAYER strikes up a sentimental tune
while BISHOP sets up two chairs, gets a glass,
then drunkenly joins in the chorus.*

PIANO PLAYER: (*singing*)
 *Thinking of December nights
 In the clear Canadian cold,
 Where the winter air don't smell bad,
 And the wind don't make you old.*

Where the rain don't wash your heart out,
And the nights ain't filled with fear.
O those old familiar voices
Whisper in my ears.

  Chorus

O Canada,
Sing a song for me.
Sing one for your lonely son,
So far across the sea.

> The PIANO PLAYER breaks into a fast-stride
> dance tune. BISHOP's reverie is interrupted by a
> drunken, half-mad Scottish AIRMAN. (He can be
> portrayed as Cockney – substitute "bloke" for
> "mate.") BISHOP, as always, plays both parts.

AIRMAN:

Ye don't fancy the Cavalry then, eh mate?

BISHOP:

What?!

AIRMAN:

I said, ye don't fancy the Cavalry then. It's worse at the
front, mate. There ye got Heinie shootin' at ye ... with
machine guns. DAKAKAKAKAK! Har, har! It's a bloody
shooting gallery with you in the middle of it, mate.

BISHOP:

This is awful. Something must be done. Jeez, I was a
casualty in training!

AIRMAN:

Take a word of advice from me, mate. The only way out ...
is up.

BISHOP:

Up?

AIRMAN:

Up. Join the Royal Flying Corps. I did. I used to be in the
Cavalry. I joined the RFC, and I like it. It's good, clean work.
Mind you, the machines barely stay in the air an' the life
expectancy of the new lads is about eleven days, but I like
it. It's good, clean work.

BISHOP:

Just a minute. How can I get into the Royal Flying Corps?
I'm Canadian. I'm cannon fodder. You have to practically
own your own plane to join the RFC.

AIRMAN:

Au contraire, mate. Au contraire. The upper classes are
depressed by the present statistics, so they're not joining
with their usual alacrity. Now anyone who wants to can get
blown out of the air. Even Canadians.

BISHOP:

Well, what do I have to do?

AIRMAN:

Ye go down, see them at the War Office – daft bunch of
twits, but they're all right. Now you act real eager, see? Like
you crave the excitement, any old rubbish. But they're not
going to know what to ask you because they don't know a

bleeding thing about it. So they'll ask you whatever comes
into their heads, which isn't much, then they'll say you
can't be a pilot, you got to be an observer.

BISHOP:

What's an observer?

AIRMAN:

He's the mate who goes along for the ride. Looks about.

BISHOP:

Oh.

AIRMAN:

Now you act real disappointed – like your mum always
wanted you to be a pilot. Then you get your transfer ...

BISHOP:

Just a minute, just a minute. So I'm an observer. I'm the guy
that looks about. So what? How do I get to be a pilot?

AIRMAN:

(*thinks about this*) I dunno. Sooner or later you just get to be
a pilot. Plenty of vacancies these days. Check the casualty
lists, wait for a bad one. (*He becomes inexplicably enraged.*)
You have to go in by the back door, you know what I mean?
Nobody gets to be a pilot right away – 'specially not fucking
Canadians!

> *The music stops cold. BISHOP speaks to
> the audience.*

BISHOP:

Did you ever trust your entire future to a drunken conversation in a bar? Two days later, I went down to see them at the War Office.

The PIANO PLAYER plays a martial intro as BISHOP faces SIR HUGH CECIL at the War Office. SIR HUGH is getting on in years and the technology of modern war has confused him.

SIR HUGH:

So. You wish to transfer to the Royal Flying Corps. Am I right? Am I correct?

BISHOP:

Yes, sir. I want to become a fighter pilot, sir.

SIR HUGH:

I thought as much. Well done. Jolly good.

BISHOP:

It's what my mother always wanted, sir.

SIR HUGH:

It's what your mother always ... oh. (*impressed*) Oh. Oh I see. Well, the situation is this, Bishop. We need good men in the Royal Flying Corps, but they must have the correct ... er, qualifications. Now while the War Office has not yet ascertained what qualifications are indeed necessary for flying a ... er ... an aeroplane, we must see to it that all candidates possess the correct qualifications – should the War Office ever decide what those qualifications ... are. Do you understand that, Bishop?

BISHOP:

Perfectly, sir.

SIR HUGH:

Jolly good. Excellent. Well done. That's more than I can say. Shall we begin, then?

BISHOP:

Ready when you are, sir.

SIR HUGH:

Oh, that's good, too! Shows keenness, you see. Excellent. Well done. Jolly good. (*aside*) Good lord, what on earth should I ask him? (*pause while he collects his thoughts; finally*) Do you ski?

BISHOP:

(*nonplussed*) Ski, sir?

SIR HUGH:

Yes. Do you ski?

BISHOP:

(*to the audience*) Here was an Englishman asking a Canadian whether or not he skied. Now if the Canadian said he didn't ski, the Englishman might find that somewhat ... suspicious. (*to SIR HUGH*) Ski, sir? Yes, sir! (*to the audience*) Never skied in my life.

SIR HUGH:

Thought you might. Well done. Excellent ... Oh dear .... (*thinks up another question*) Do you ride a horse?

BISHOP:

I'm an officer in the Cavalry, sir!

SIR HUGH:

Doesn't necessarily follow. But let's put down that you ride, shall we? Now what about sports? Run, jump, throw the ball, play the game, eh what?

BISHOP:

Sports, sir? All sports!

SIR HUGH:

Oh, I say! Bishop, I am most impressed!

BISHOP:

Does this mean I can become a fighter pilot, sir?

SIR HUGH:

Who knows, Bishop? Who knows? All full-up with fighter pilots at the moment, I'm afraid. Takes six months, a year to get in. Terribly sorry, old man. Nothing I can do.

BISHOP:

I see, sir.

SIR HUGH:

However: we have an immediate need for observers – you know, that's the fellow who goes along for the ride. Looks about, I suppose. What do you say, Bishop?

BISHOP:

(*to the audience*) I thought about it. I wanted to be a pilot. I couldn't. So in the fall of 1915, I joined the Twenty-One Squadron as an observer. You see, that's what they were using the machines for at that time. Observation. You could take pictures of enemy troop formations, direct artillery fire, stuff like that. And I was really good at the aerial photography. I've got these great eyes – remember?

The PIANO PLAYER reprises the ethereal "flying" theme.

BISHOP:

And to fly! You're in this old Farnham trainer. Sounds like a tractor. Coughs, wheezes, chugs its way up to one thousand feet. You're in a kite with a motor that can barely get off the ground – but even so, you're in the air. You're not ... on the ground. You're above everything.

The ethereal piano theme becomes carnivalesque.

It was a different world up there, a different war. And a different breed of men fighting that war. Flyers! During training we heard all the stories: if you went down behind enemy lines and were killed, they'd come over – the Germans, that is – under a flag of truce, and drop a photograph of your grave. Nice. If you were taken prisoner, it was the champagne razzle in the mess, talking and drinking all night. It was a different war they were fighting up there – and from where I stood it looked pretty darn good!

The PIANO PLAYER introduces a mess-hall singalong song reminiscent of Flanders and Swann.

PIANO PLAYER:

Could you be a tiny bit more specific, please?

BISHOP:

Certainly.

BISHOP & PIANO PLAYER: (*speaking alternate lines, then singing together for the chorus*)

> I see two planes in the air,
> A fight that's fair and square,
> With dips and loops and rolls
> That would scare ya. (I'm scared already.)
> We will force the German down,
> And arrest him on the ground,
> A patriotic lad from Bavaria. (Jawohl!)
>
> He'll surrender willingly,
> And salute our chivalry,
> For this war was none of our creation.
> (Damn right about that.)
> But before it's prison camp,
> And a bed that's cold and damp,
> We'll have a little celebration.

> *Chorus*

> *O we'll toast our youth*
> *On champagne and vermouth,*
> *For all of us know what it's like to fly.*
> *O the fortunes of war*
> *Can't erase esprit de corps,*
> *And we'll all of us be friends 'til we die.*

PIANO PLAYER:

Be so good as to elaborate on that general theme.

BISHOP:

I shall do so. (*singing*)

O we'll drink the night away,
And when the Bosch is led away,
We'll load him down with cigarettes and wine.
(Of course we will.)

Both sing.

BISHOP & PIANO PLAYER: (*singing*)

We'll drink a final toast goodbye,
But for the grace of God go I,
And we'll vow that we'll be friends ... another time.

Chorus

O we'll toast our youth
On champagne and vermouth,
For all of us know what it's like to fly.
O the fortunes of war
Can't erase esprit de corps
And we'll all of us be friends 'til we die.

BISHOP:

You want chivalry? You want gallantry? You want nice
guys? Well, that's your flyer – and, jeez, I was going to be
one of them!

The PIANO PLAYER returns to the carnival theme.

51

BISHOP:

January 1st, 1916, I crossed the Channel as a flyer ... well, an observer, anyway. And that's when I found out that Twenty-One Squadron was known as the "suicide squadron." That awful nickname preyed on my mind, you know?

The carnival theme darkens.

And the Archies? The anti-aircraft guns? (*shudders*) Not tonight, Archibald! You're tooling around over the line, doing your observation work, a sitting duck, when suddenly you're surrounded by these little black puffs of smoke ... Then bam! Whiz! Shrapnel shrieking all around you. I was hit on the head by a piece of shrapnel – just a bruise, but a couple of inches lower and I could have been killed. And we were all scared stiff of this new German machine – the Fokker. It had this interrupter gear, so the pilot could shoot straight through the propeller without actually shooting the propeller off – all he had to do was aim his plane at you!

Carnival music dies.

And casualties? Lots and lots and lots of casualties. It was a grim situation – but we didn't know how grim it could get until we saw the R.E.7. The Reconnaissance Experimental Number Seven: our new plane.

BISHOP mimes the following, using furniture and whatever props are at hand.

To look at it, what you saw was a mound of cables and wires, with a thousand pounds of equipment hanging on to it. Four machine guns. A five-hundred-pound bomb, for God's sake! Cameras, reconnaissance equipment ... Roger Neville (that's my pilot), he and I are ordered into the thing to take it up. (*imitates a sputtering, floundering airplane that will not fly*) Of course, the thing doesn't get off the ground. Anyone could see that. We think fine, good riddance – uh-oh. The officers go into a huddle.

OFFICER ONE:

Well, what do you think the problem is?

OFFICER TWO:

I don't know, sir. Maybe we should try taking the bomb off.

OFFICER ONE:

A splendid idea. Take the bomb off.

OFFICER TWO:

Take the bomb off!

PIANO PLAYER:

Take the bomb off!

BISHOP:

Take the bomb off! So we take the bomb off and try again. This time the thing sort of flops down the runway like a crippled duck. (*imitates the floundering airplane*) Finally, by taking everything off but one machine gun, the thing sort of flopped itself into the air and chugged along. It was a pig. We were all scared stiff of it. So they put us on active duty – as *bombers*! They give us two bombs each, tell us to fly over Hunland and drop them on somebody. But in order to accommodate for the weight of the bombs? They took our machine gun away!

The PIANO PLAYER breaks into a sort of
ragtime blues.

Dearest Margaret. We are dropping bombs on the enemy from unarmed machines. It is exciting work. It's hard to keep your confidence in a war when you don't have a gun. Somehow we get back in one piece and we start joking around and inspecting the machine for shrapnel damage. You're so thankful not to be dead. Then you go back to the barracks and lie down ... and a kind of terrible loneliness comes over you. It's like waiting for the firing squad. You want to cry, you feel so frightened, and so alone. I think all of us who aren't dead think these things. Thinking of you constantly, I remain ...

BISHOP takes a rest while the
PIANO PLAYER sings.

PIANO PLAYER: (*singing*)
  Nobody shoots no one in Canada,
  At least nobody they don't know.
  Nobody shoots no one in Canada,
  Last battle was a long, long time ago.

  Nobody picks no fights in Canada,
  Not with nobody they ain't met.
  Nobody starts no wars in Canada,
  Folks tend to work for what they get.

BISHOP joins in.

BISHOP & PIANO PLAYER: (*singing*)

Take me under
That big blue sky,
Where the deer and the black bear play.
May not be heaven,
But heaven knows we try,
Wish I was in Canada today.

Nobody drops no bombs on Canada,
Don't want no one to go to hell.
Nobody drops no bombs on Canada,
Where folks tend to wish each other well.

The music continues under the following. Music is interrupted by sound effects where appropriate.

BISHOP:

Of course, in this situation it wasn't long before the accidents started happening again. You know, it's kind of spooky, but I think being accident-prone actually saved my life. I'm driving a truckload of parts a couple of miles from the aerodrome and I run into another truck. (*crash!*) I'm inspecting the undercarriage of my machine when a cable snaps (*ping!*) and hits me on the head. I'm unconscious for two days. I had a tooth pulled? It got infected. I was in the hospital for two weeks. Then Roger does this really bad landing. (*crash!*) I hit my knee on a metal brace inside the plane so hard I could barely walk! Then I got three weeks in London, none too soon. On the boat back to England we all got into the champagne and cognac pretty heavy, and by the time we arrived we were all pretty tight, and this game developed, to see who would be the first to touch foot on English soil. I'm leading the race down the gangplank, and I trip and fall. (*multiple crashes!*) Everyone else falls on top of me – right on the knee I hurt in the crash! God, the pain was awful. But I'd be damned if I'd spend my leave in the hospital, so I just poured down the brandy until the thing was pretty well numb, had a hell of a time. If the pain got to me in the night and I couldn't sleep, I'd just pour down the brandy. But around my last day of leave, I started thinking about the bombing runs, the Archies, the Fokkers, and I thought, jeez, maybe I better have someone look at this knee! The doctor found I had a cracked kneecap, which meant I'd be in the hospital for a couple of weeks. But he also found that I had a badly strained heart, which meant I would be in the hospital for an indefinite period. As far as I was concerned, I was out of the war.

BISHOP & PIANO PLAYER: (*singing*)
> *Take me under*
> *That big blue sky,*
> *Where the deer and the black bear play.*
> *May not be heaven,*
> *But heaven knows we try,*
> *Wish I was in Canada today.*
>
> *I'm dreaming of the trees in Canada,*
> *Northern lights are dancing in my head.*
> *If I die, then let me die in Canada,*
> *Where there's a chance I'll die in bed.*

The music becomes restful.

BISHOP:

The hospital is nice. People don't shoot at you. People don't drop things on you. I thought it would be a nice place to spend the war. I went to sleep for three days.

A crash on piano, followed by distorted marching music.

I had this nightmare. A terrible dream. I am in the lobby of the Grand Hotel in London. The band is playing military music, and the lobby is full of English and German officers, and they're dancing – together. And their medals jingle like sleigh bells in the snow – Ching-ching! Ching-ching! Ching-ching! The sound is deafening. I've got to get out of there. I start to run, but my knee gives out underneath me. As I get up, I get kicked in the stomach by a Prussian boot. As I turn to run, I get kicked in the rear by an English boot. Then I turn around, and all the officers have formed a chorus line, like the Follies, and they are heading for me – kicking! I scream as a hundred boots kick me high in the air, as I turn over and over in the air, shouting, "Help me! Help me! They're trying to kill me!"

The music reaches a climax. He stops abruptly when he hears a voice.

LADY ST. HELIER:

My goodness, Bishop, you'll not get any rest screaming at the top of your lungs like that.

BISHOP:

In front of me was a face I'd never seen before – very old, female, with long white hair pulled back tightly in a bun, exposing two of the largest ears I had ever seen.

LADY ST. HELIER:

You would be the son of Will Bishop of Owen Sound, Canada, would you not? Of course you are – the resemblance is quite startling. Your father was a loyal supporter of a very good friend of mine – Sir Wilfrid Laurier. It was in that connection that I first met your father in Ottawa ... A gaping mouth is most impolite, Bishop. No, I am not a clairvoyant. I am Lady St. Helier: Reform alderman, poetess, friend of Churchill, and the woman who will save your life.

BISHOP:

(*speechless*) Er, um ... I mean, ahhh ...

LADY ST. HELIER:

Enough of this gay banter, Bishop. Time runs apace and my life is not without its limits. You have been making rather a mess of it, haven't you? You're a rude young man behaving like cannon fodder. Perfectly acceptable characteristics in a Canadian – but you are different. You are a gifted Canadian. And that gift belongs to a much older and deeper tradition than Canada can ever provide. Quite against your own wishes, you will be released from this wretched hospital in two weeks' time. Promptly at three o'clock on that afternoon, you will present yourself before my door at Portland Place, dressed for tea and in a positive frame of mind. Please be punctual. Good day, Mr. Bishop.

BISHOP:

(*to the audience*) Well, jeez, that old girl must have known something I didn't, because two weeks later I find myself in front of her door at Portland Place, in my best uniform, shining my shoes on my trousers. (*He mimes knocking on the door, which creaks open. He looks up – way up.*) Hi.

> *CEDRIC the butler looks down at him with distaste.*

CEDRIC:

Madam. The colonial is here. Shall I show him in?

LADY ST. HELIER:

(*muffled in the distance*) Yes, Cedric, please. Show him in.

CEDRIC:

Get in.

BISHOP:

I'm shown into the largest room I have ever seen. A fireplace eight feet high; a staircase that must have had a hundred steps in it. I'm not used to dealing with nobility: servants, grand ballrooms, pheasant hunting on the heath, fifty-year-old brandy over billiards, breakfast in bed – shit, what a life!

CEDRIC:

Madam is in the study. Get in.

BISHOP:

The study: books, books, more books than I'll ever read. Persian rug. Tiger's head over the mantel. African spears in

the corner. (*sings*) *"Rule Britannia, Britannia rules the ..."*
I stood at the door. I'm on edge. Out of my element.

LADY ST. HELIER:

Very punctual, Mr. Bishop. Please sit down.

BISHOP:

I sit in this chair that is all carved lions ... (*winces*) One of
the lions stuck in my back.

CEDRIC:

Would our visitor from Canada care for tea, Madam?

LADY ST. HELIER:

Would you care for something to drink, Bishop?

BISHOP:

(*unenthusiastic*) Tea? Ahhh, sure. Tea would be fine.

LADY ST. HELIER:

A tea for Bishop, Cedric. And I'll have a gin.

BISHOP:

Gin? I wonder if I might change mine to ... (*notes CEDRIC's
intimidating presence*) No, no, no, tea would be, tea would
be fine. (*to the audience*) Tea is served. I sip my tea. Lady
St. Helier sips her gin. And Cedric looms over me – afraid I
was going to drool on the rug or something. Lady St. Helier
stared at me through these thick spectacles. Then suddenly
her ears twitched, like she was honing in on something.

LADY ST. HELIER:

I have written a poem in your honour, Bishop. I can but
hope that your rustic mind will appreciate its significance.
(*to the PIANO PLAYER*) Cedric!

> *She performs a recitative to piano
> accompaniment.*

You're a typical Canadian,
You're modesty itself,
And you really wouldn't want to hurt a flea.
But you're just about to go
The way of the buffalo.
You'd do well to take this good advice from me.

I'm awfully sick and tired,
Being constantly required
To stand by and watch Canadians make the best of it;
For the colonial mentality
Defies all rationality,
You seem to go to lengths to make a mess of it.

Why don't you grow up,
Before I throw up?
Do you expect somebody else to do it for you?
Before you're dead out,
Get the lead out,
And seize what little life still lies before you.

Do you really expect Empire
To settle back, retire,
And say, "Colonials, go on your merry way"?

I'm very tired of your whining
And your infantile maligning,
Your own weakness simply won't be whined away.

O don't be so naive,
And take your heart off your sleeve,
For a fool and his life will soon be parted;
War's a fact of life today,
And it will not be wished away,
Forget that fact and you are dead before you've started.

So, Bishop, grow up
Before I throw up.
Your worst enemy is yourself, as you well know.
Before you're dead out,
Get the lead out,
You have your own naivety to overthrow.

> *The PIANO PLAYER ends with a flourish.*

LADY ST. HELIER:

(*to the PIANO PLAYER*) Thank you, Cedric. (*to BISHOP*)
Do I make myself clear, Mr. Bishop? You will cease this
mediocrity that your record only too clearly reveals. You
will become the pilot that you wished to be – and were
lamentably content to settle for less. Now this will take
time, for you must recover the health that you have so
seriously undermined. To that end, you will become a
lodger at Portland Place – top of the stairs, third floor,
seventh door on the left. (*to CEDRIC*) Cedric, be kind to
Bishop. And ignore his bad manners. For cultivation exacts
a price – the loss of a certain vitality. Beneath this rude

colonial exterior there beats a power you will never know. Properly harnessed, that power will win wars for you. Churchill knows it, and I know it, too. (*to BISHOP*) Good day, Mr. Bishop.

A pause while BISHOP digests this.

BISHOP:

(*to the audience*) Now there are one or two Canadians who would have taken offence at that. (*pause*) Not me. Staying at Portland Place, I found out some things right away – for example, life goes much smoother when you have influence. Take this pilot business, for example. Lady St. Helier gets on the phone to Churchill himself. The very next day I'm called down to the War Office. The atmosphere is much different.

The PIANO PLAYER plays a martial intro as once again BISHOP faces SIR HUGH CECIL.

SIR HUGH:

Bishop! Jolly good, well done, excellent, good to see you! Well, my boy, your mother's wish is finally going to come true.

BISHOP:

Oh really, sir?

SIR HUGH:

Yes, yes, you are going to become a pilot. No problem, pas de problème. Medical examination in two days' time, then report for training.

BISHOP:

(*to the audience*) Medical examination!? What about my
weak heart? What about the fact that two weeks ago I was
on the verge of medical discharge?

> *An overworked, preoccupied DOCTOR deals with*
> *his case.*

DOCTOR:

Ah yes, Bishop – strip to the waist. Good. Stick out your
tongue and say ninety-nine – good. (*inserts finger below*)
Cough twice – that's good, too. Now turn around ten
times – eight ... nine ... ten ... Attention! Still on your feet,
Bishop? You're fit as a fiddle and ready to fly!

> *The PIANO PLAYER plays a kind of polka. BISHOP*
> *sings a merry tune with macabre overtones.*

BISHOP: (*singing*)
> *Gonna fly ...*
> *Gonna fly so high*
> *Like a bird in the sky,*
> *With the wind in my hair*
> *And the sun burning in my eyes.*
> *Flying Canadian,*
> *Machine gun in my hand,*
> *First Hun I see's the first Hun to die.*
>
> *Gonna fly ...*
> *In my machine*
> *Gonna shoot so clean,*
> *Gonna hear them scream*

When I hit them between the eyes.
Flying Canadian,
Machine gun in my hand,
First Hun I see's the first Hun to die.

Chorus

Flying …
What have I been waiting for?
What a way to fight a war!
Flying Canadian,
Machine gun in my hand,
First Hun I see's the first Hun to die.

Gonna fly …
Gonna shoot them down
'Til they hit the ground,
And they burn with the sound
Of bacon on the fry. (Sssss!)

Flying Canadian,
Machine gun in my hand,
First Hun I see's the first Hun to die.

Chorus

Flying …
What have I been waiting for?
What a way to fight a war!
Flying Canadian,
Machine gun in my hand,
First Hun I see's the first Hun to die.

*The song ends abruptly, then BISHOP launches
into a sequence that can be done in many
different ways, all of which – whether using an
ashtray, a model plane, or some other device
– involve a good deal of mime; as well, BISHOP
performs sound effects vocally, much as a boy of
about age ten might do.*

BISHOP:

I'll never forget my first solo flight. Lonely? Jesus. You're
sitting at the controls, all by yourself – trying to remember
what they're all for. Everyone has stopped doing what they're
doing – to watch you. There's an ambulance parked across
the field – with its engines running, you know why. You also
know that there's a surgical team in the hospital, just ready
to rip.

PIANO PLAYER:

Switch off!

BISHOP:

(*at the controls*) Switch off.

PIANO PLAYER:

Petrol on!

BISHOP:

Petrol on.

PIANO PLAYER:

Suck in!

BISHOP:

Suck in.

PIANO PLAYER:

Switch on!

BISHOP:

Switch on.

PIANO PLAYER:

Contact!

BISHOP:

Contact! The propeller is given a sharp turn and the engine starts with a roar. (*He makes an engine sound, then coughs.*) Coughs a few times, then starts hitting on all cylinders. (*steady engine noise*) You signal for them to take away the chocks. Then you're bouncing across the field, under your own power, and head her up into the wind. (*checks his foot controls*) Rudder. (*click, click*) Elevators. (*click, click*) Ailerons. (*squeak, squeak*) Heart. (*ba-BOOM! ba-BOOM! ba-BOOM!*) I open the throttle all the way (*engine accelerates*) ... and you're off! Pull back on the stick – easy – easy! (*He demonstrates as the plane bumps violently along, then finally becomes airborne.*) Once I was in the air, I felt a lot better. In fact, I felt like a king! Mind you, I'm not fooling around. I'm flying straight as I can, climbing steadily. (*looks about*) All by yourself! What a feeling! ... (*looks down, becomes alarmed*) I've got to turn! I execute a gentle turn ... skidding like crazy, but what the hell. I bank it a little more – too much, too much! ... But all in all, I'm having a hell of a time – until I remember I've to land! What do I do now? Keep your head, that's what you do now. Pull back on the throttle. (*engine has a coughing fit*) Too much! I put the nose down into a steep dive ... too steep! I bring it up again, down again, up, down ... and in a series of steps, I descend to earth. Then I execute everything I remember you have to do to make a perfect landing ... forty feet off the ground! I put the nose down and do another perfect landing ... This time, I'm only eight feet off the ground. But now I have no room left to do another nose-down manoeuvre. The rumpty takes things into her own hands and just pancakes the rest of the way to the ground. (*piano crashes*) First solo flight! Greatest day in a man's life!

BISHOP & PIANO PLAYER: (*singing*)
>   *Flying ...*
>   *What have I been waiting for?*
>   *What a way to fight a war.*
>
>   *Flying Canadian,*
>   *Machine gun in my hand,*
>   *First Hun I see's the first Hun to die.*

>   *The song ends abruptly.*

FOR A YOUNG ACTOR / FOR AN OLD ACTOR

>   *When BISHOP is portrayed as an old man, the following scene is deleted entirely, from "In the early part of 1916" to "Then came March 25th, 1917," the principal reason being that Bishop's tendency to error has been well established. By moving from his first solo flight directly to his first kill, there is a continuum to the old man's memory. With the younger BISHOP, however, there is value in reminding the audience that*

his future status was by no means a foregone
conclusion, that a superior officer could justifiably
regard him as a jackass.

BISHOP:

In the early part of 1916, I was posted back to France – as
a fighter pilot. Sixty Squadron, Third British Brigade. I
worked like a Trojan for those wings – and I just about
lost them before I really began. I was returning from my
first O.P. – Operational Patrol – and I crashed my Nieuport
on landing. I wasn't hurt, but the aircraft was pretty well
pranged, and that was bad because General John Higgins,
the Brigade Commander, saw me do it. Well, he couldn't
help but see me do it. I just about crashed at his feet!

HIGGINS:

I watched you yesterday, Bishop. You destroyed a machine
– a very expensive, very nice machine. Doing a simple
landing on a clear day. That machine was more valuable
than you'll ever be, bucko.

BISHOP:

Sir, it was a gust of wind from the hangar. Ask Major Scott,
our patrol leader, it could have happened to anyone ...

HIGGINS:

Bishop, I was on the field.

BISHOP:

Yes, sir.

HIGGINS:

There was no wind.

BISHOP:

No wind. Yes, sir.

HIGGINS:

I have your record here before me, Bishop. It's not a very impressive document, is it? On the positive side ... you were wounded. And you scored well in target practice, without having ever actually fired upon the enemy. The list of your negative accomplishments, however, is longer, isn't it? Much longer. Conduct unbecoming an officer, breaches of discipline, a lot of silly accidents – suspicious accidents, if I might say so – a trail of wrecked machinery in your wake! You are a terrible pilot, Bishop, and a liability to the RFC, and I wish to God you were back in Canada where you belong – or failing that, digging a trench in some unstrategic valley. In short, you're finished, Bishop, finished! When your replacement arrives, he will replace you. That is all.

BISHOP:

(*to the audience*) That was the lowest point in my career. Then came March 25th, 1917.

> *The following scene is performed with BISHOP creating the sound effects in the manner of his first solo flight, but with a growing sense of menace, as a boy's adventure story takes on real adult fear and aggression, and as the adrenalin rush takes over.*

Four Nieuport scouts in diamond formation climb to nine thousand feet, crossing the line somewhere between Arras and St. Léger. Our patrol is to crisscross the lines, noting Heinie's positions and troop movements.

The drone of an airplane.

I'm the last man in the patrol – tough place to be because, if you fall too far behind, the headhunters are waiting for you. It starts out cloudy, then gradually clears up. We fly for half an hour and don't see anything, just miles and miles of nothing.

The drone continues – then a warning chord on piano.

Suddenly, I see four specks, above and behind us – perfect place for an enemy attack. I watch as the specks get larger … I can make out the black crosses – Huns!

The piano underscore becomes more rhythmic – like the approaching torpedo earlier in Act One.

It's hard to believe that they are real, and alive – and hostile. I want to circle around and have a better look at them. Albatros V-Strutters, beautiful with their sweptback planes, powerful and quick. RRRrrr. We keep flying steadily – Jack Scott, our leader, either hasn't seen them or wants them to think he hasn't seen them. They're getting closer and closer. We keep flying straight. They're two hundred yards behind us, getting closer and closer …

The piano follows the action like a movie score.

Suddenly, Rrrr! Jack Scott opens up into a sharp, climbing turn to get above and behind them. (*gesturing*) The rest of us follow – Rrrr! Rrrr! Rrrrr! I'm slower than the rest and come out about forty yards behind. Ahead of me a dogfight is happening right in front of my very eyes, real pandemonium, planes turning every which way – Rrrr! Rrrr! Machine-gun fire – AKAKAKAK!

> *The piano underscore becomes surreal and discordant.*

Suddenly – Rrrr! Jack Scott sweeps below me with an Albatros on his tail, raking his wings and fuselage with gunfire! For a moment I'm just frozen there, not knowing what to do, my whole body just shaking! ... Then I throw the stick forward and dive on the Hun. I keep him in my Aldis sight until he completely fills the lens – AKAKAKAK! What a feeling, as he flips onto his back and falls out of control ...

> *The piano stops cold.*

But wait! Wait! Grid Caldwell told me about this. He's not out of control, he's faking it! He's going to level out at two thousand feet and escape. Bastard!

> *Battle music resumes.*

I dive after him with my engine full on. Sure enough, he comes out of it, but I'm still there – AKAKAKAK! Again, my tracers smash into his machine – God, I've got to be hitting him! He flips over on his back and is gone again,

but this time I'm right on him. EEEEEEEEE! The wires on
my machine scream in protest. Nieuports have had their
wings come off at 150 miles an hour, I must be doing 180,
I just don't give a shit! I keep firing on the tumbling Hun –
AKAKAKAKAAK!

Huge crash on piano.

He just crashes into the earth and explodes in flames! BAA-
WHOOSH! I pull back on the stick and level out, screaming
at the top of my lungs – I WIN, I WIN, I WIN!

Abrupt silence, followed by the sound of wind.
No engine, no nothing.

Jesus, my engine stopped! It must have filled with oil on
the dive. I try every trick in the book to get it going again.
Nothing. Oh God, I'm going to go in!

Gunfire from the PIANO PLAYER.

Ground fire! I must still be over Hunland. Just my luck to
do something right and end up being taken prisoner. Lower
and lower. I pick out what seems to be a level patch and I
put her down.

The plane lands with a bouncing crash. BISHOP
ends up on the floor, crouched behind a prop or
a piece of furniture.

I got out of the plane into what seemed to be a shell hole.
I took my Very-Light pistol with me. I wasn't exactly sure
what I was going to do with it ...

TOMMY:

(*in a Newfoundland accent*) Well, you're just in time for a cup
of tea there, my son.

BISHOP:

(*panic*) Arrgh! (*relieved*) Jeez, you speak English! Hey, look,
where am I?

TOMMY:

Yer at the bottom of Signal Hill in downtown St. John's.
You want to keep down, duckie? Heinie's just over there.
Well gol, that was a nice bit of flying you did there – yer a
hundred yards our side of the line.

BISHOP:

Look, can you do me a favour? I'd like to try and get the
plane up again.

TOMMY:

Not tonight, my son. No, you're going to have to take the
Bridal Suite here at the Avalon Hotel.

> *The shriek of shelling and the crash of explosions
> get louder.*

BISHOP:

I spent the night in a trench, in six inches of water. (*shriek!
crash!*) The Tommies seemed to be able to sleep. I sure
couldn't.

*The barrage reaches a peak, then fades into the
distance.*

Next morning at first light, I crawled out to see how my
plane was. Miraculously, it hadn't been hurt ... And that's
when I got my first look at no man's land. Jesus, what a
mess. Hardly a tree left standing – and the smell! It was
hard to believe you were still on earth. I saw a couple of
Tommies sleeping in a trench nearby. (*to the Tommies*) Hey,
you guys. I wonder if you could give me a hand with ...

*The Tommies aren't sleeping. He recoils from
what he sees.*

Oh my God.

*The PIANO PLAYER begins to sing.
BISHOP joins in.*

BISHOP & PIANO PLAYER: (*singing*)
*O the bloody earth is littered
With the fighters and the quitters,
O what could be more bitter
Than a nameless death below;
See the trenches, long and winding,
See the battle, slowly grinding,
Don't you wonder how good men can live so low.*

*Up above the sun is burning,
Up above the clouds are turning,
You can hear those soldiers yearning:
"O if only I could fly!"*

From the burning sun, I'll sight you,
In the burning sun, I'll fight you –
O let us dance together in the sky.

    Chorus

In the sky,
In the sky,
Just you and I up there together –
Who knows why?
One the hunter, one the hunted,
A life to live, a death confronted –
"O let us dance together in the sky."

For you the bell is ringing,
And for you the bullets stinging,
My Lewis gun is singing –
O my friend, it's you or I!
And I'll watch your last returning
To the earth, the fire burning,
Look up and you will see me wave goodbye.

    Chorus

In the sky,
In the sky,
Just you and I up there together –
Who knows why?
One the hunter, one the hunted,
A life to live, a death confronted –
O let us dance together in the sky.

ACT TWO

*The PIANO PLAYER plays and sings "The Bold
Aviator." This mordant little song (the lyrics are
authentic from the period) can be performed
as a drinking song, as a singalong, or as a
plaintive ballad.*

PIANO PLAYER: (*singing*)
*O the bold aviator lay dying,
As 'neath the wreckage he lay,
To the sobbing mechanic beside him
These last parting words he did say:*

*"Two valves you'll find in my stomach,
Three sparkplugs are safe in my lung;
The prop is in splinters inside me,
To my fingers, the joystick has clung.*

*Then get you six brandies and sodas,
And lay them all out in a row;
And get you six other good airmen
To drink to this pilot below.*

*Take the cylinders out of my kidneys,
The connecting rod out of my brain;
From the small of my back take the crankshaft,
And assemble the engine again."*

*The song ends. Immediately the PIANO PLAYER
launches into the "Survival" theme, as a much-
altered BISHOP speaks as though giving advice to
a novice pilot.*

BISHOP:

Survival. That's the important thing. And the only way to
learn survival – is to survive. Success depends on accuracy
and surprise: how well you shoot, how you get into the
fight, and how well you fly – in that order. I can't fly worth
a shit compared to someone like Barker or Ball, but I don't
care. If I get a kill, it's usually in the first few seconds. Any
longer than that, and you might as well get the hell out.
You've got to be good enough to get him in the first few
bursts; so practise your shooting as much as you can – after
patrols, between patrols, on your day off. If I get a clear shot
at a guy, he's dead. Ever heard of "flamers"? That's when
you bounce a machine and it just bursts into flames. Now
I don't want to sound bloodthirsty or anything, but when
that happens, it's very satisfying. But it's almost always
pure luck, you hit a gas line or something like that. If you
want the machine to go down every time, you aim for one
thing – the man. I always go for the man.

*The music stops and the PIANO PLAYER takes the
part of the M.C. in a French cabaret.*

PIANO PLAYER:

(*French accent*) Ladies and Gentlemen. Mesdames et
Messieurs. Charlie's Bar, Amiens, proudly presents …
Ze Lovely Hélène!

*BISHOP takes the part of a Dietrich-like cabaret
singer. He and the PIANO PLAYER sing.*

HÉLÈNE:

> *Johnny was a Christian, he was humble and humane,*
> *His conscience was clear and his soul without a stain;*

PIANO PLAYER:

> *He was contemplating heaven when –*

HÉLÈNE:

> *– ze wings fell off his plane.*

PIANO PLAYER:

> *And he never got out alive?*

HÉLÈNE:

> *Non. He did not survive.*
>
> *George was patriotic, his country he adored,*
> *He was the first to volunteer when his*
>   *land took up the sword;*

PIANO PLAYER:

> *And a half a dozen medals were –*

HÉLÈNE:

> *His posthumous reward.*

PIANO PLAYER:

> *And he never got out alive?*

HÉLÈNE:

> *Non. He did not survive.*

They sing chorus together.

HÉLÈNE & PIANO PLAYER:

> *So when you fight, stay as calm as the ocean,*
> *And watch what's going on behind your shoulder;*
> *Remember, war's not the place for deep emotion –*

HÉLÈNE:

> *And maybe you'll get ... a little older.*

> *The "Survivial" theme resumes. BISHOP, as*
> *himself, continues the lesson.*

BISHOP:

> Come into a fight with an advantage – height, speed,
> surprise. Come at him out of the sun, he'll never see
> you. Get on his tail, his blind spot, so you can shoot him
> without too much risk to yourself. Generally, patrols don't
> watch behind them as much, so sneak up on the last man,
> he'll never know what hit him ... Hunt them! Like Hell's
> handmaiden! If it's one on one, you come at the bugger,
> guns blazing, he chickens out, and you get him as he comes
> across your sights. If you both veer the same way ... you're
> dead. So it's tricky. You have to keep your nerve.

> *The song resumes.*

HÉLÈNE:

> *Geoffrey made a virtue out of cowardice and fear,*
> *The first to go on sick leave and the last to volunteer –*

PIANO PLAYER:

> *He was running from a fight –*

HÉLÈNE:

> *When they attacked him from the rear.*

PIANO PLAYER:

> *And he never got out alive?*

HÉLÈNE:

> *Non. He did not survive.*

> > *Back to the "Survival" theme. BISHOP resumes the lesson.*

BISHOP:

> The other thing is your mental attitude. It's not like the infantry, where a bunch of guys work themselves up into a screaming rage and tear off over the top, yelling and waving their bayonets – it's not like that. You're part of a machine, so you have to stay very calm and cold, so that you and your machine work together to bring the other fellow down. You get so you don't feel anything after a while ... until the moment you start firing, then that old dry-throat, heart-throbbing thrill comes back. It's a great feeling!

> > *BISHOP sings as the LOVELY HÉLÈNE.*

HÉLÈNE:

> *Jimmy hated Germans with a passion cold and deep,*
> *He cursed them when he saw them, he*
> > *cursed them in his sleep –*

PIANO PLAYER:

He was cursing when his plane went down –

HÉLÈNE:

And landed in a heap.

PIANO PLAYER:

And he never got out alive?

HÉLÈNE:

Non. He did not survive.

Both sing chorus.

HÉLÈNE & PIANO PLAYER:

So when you fight, stay as calm as the ocean,
And watch what's going on behind your shoulder;
Remember, war's not the place for deep emotion –

HÉLÈNE:

And maybe you will get … (softly) a little older.

The PIANO PLAYER plays a series of minor chords.

BISHOP:

Bloody April, we lost just about everyone I started with:
Knowles, Hall, Williams, Townsend, Chapman. Steadman
– shot down the day he joined the squadron. You see, the
Hun has better machines than ours, and some of their
pilots are very, very good. But practice makes perfect – if
you can stay alive long enough to practice. It gets easier and
easier to stay alive because hardly anyone has the same

experience as you ... (*silence*) Oh yeah, and another thing: you take your fun where you can find it.

The PIANO PLAYER begins a variation of the
"Survival" theme – slower and more gently.

He has noticed the lovely Hélène. She has noticed him. They meet outside. Without a word, she signals him to follow. Silently, they walk down an alleyway, through an archway, and up a darkened stairway. They are in her room. He watches as she lights a candle. Then she turns to him and says, "I should not be doing this. My lover is a colonel at the front. But you are so beautiful ... and so, so young." An hour later they kiss in the darkened doorway. She says, "If you see me, you do not know me." And she is gone.

He meets his friends, who have had the same good luck. It's late. They've missed the last bus to the aerodrome ... Arm in arm, they walk in the moonlight, silently sharing a flask of brandy, breathing in that warm spring air. As they approach Filescamp, they begin to sing, loudly: "Mademoiselle from Armentières, parlez-vous. Mademoiselle from Armentières, parlez-vous" ... as if to leave behind the feelings they have had that night. In an hour, they will be on patrol. They go to bed. They sleep.

Sudden crashing piano chords. PIANO PLAYER
plays "Dearest Margaret" theme as BISHOP writes
a letter to Margaret.

Dearest Margaret. It is the merry month of May, and today I sent another merry Hun to his merry death. I'm not sure you would appreciate the bloodthirsty streak that has come over me in the past months. How I hate the Hun. He has killed so many of my friends. I enjoy killing him now. I go up as much as I can, even on my day off. My score is getting higher and higher – because I like it.

Chord change on piano.

Yesterday, I had a narrow escape. A bullet came through the windshield – ping! – creased my helmet. But a miss is as good as a mile, and if I am for it, then I am for it, but I do not believe that I am for it.

Chord change.

My superiors are pleased. Not only have I been made captain, they are recommending me for the Military Cross.

Chord change.

Thinking of you constantly, I remain ...

The PIANO PLAYER segues to the "Lovely Hélène"
waltz. BISHOP speaks the verse.

You may think you've something special
    that will get you through this war,
But the odds aren't in your favour, that's
    a fact you can't ignore;

PIANO PLAYER: (*singing*)
   Chances are the man will come, knocking at your door –

BISHOP: (*singing*)

> *And you'll never get out alive.*
> *You won't survive.*

Both sing chorus.

BISHOP & PIANO PLAYER: (*singing*)

> *So when you fight, stay as calm as the ocean,*
> *And watch what's going on behind your shoulder;*
> *Remember, war's not the place for deep emotion,*
> *And maybe you will get –*

BISHOP: (*singing*)

> *A little older.*

End song. Pause, as BISHOP produces a picture, a memento of ALBERT BALL.

BISHOP:

Albert Ball, Britain's highest-scoring ace, sat before me. His black eyes gleamed at me – very pale, very intense. Back home we would have said he had eyes like two pissholes in the snow. But that's not very romantic. And Albert Ball was romantic, Jesus, if anybody was.

BISHOP performs a scene, playing himself and ALBERT BALL.

BALL:

Compatriots in glory! Oh, Bishop, I have an absolutely ripping idea. I want you to try and picture this: two pilots cross the line in the dim, early dawn. It is dark. A slight fog.

They fly straight for the German aerodromes at Douai –
ghosts in the night. The Hun, unsuspecting, sleeps cosily in
his lair. The sentries are sleeping. Perhaps the Baron von
Richthofen himself is there, sleeping, dreaming of eagles
and … Wiener schnitzel. Suddenly, he is awakened by the
sound of machine-gun fire! He rushes to his window to see
four, maybe five, of his best machines in flames! He watches
as the frantic pilots try to take off, and one by one are shot
down! The two unknown raiders strike a devastating blow!
Bishop, you and I are those two unknown raiders.

BISHOP:

Jeez, I like it! It's a good plan! (*pause*) How do we get out?

BALL:

Get out?

BISHOP:

Yeah, get out. You know – escape.

BALL:

I don't think you quite get the picture, Bishop. It's an heroic
exploit … Getting out has nothing to do with it.

BISHOP:

Oh. (*pause*) Well, it's a good plan. It's got a few holes I'd like
to see plugged. I'd like to think about it.

BALL:

All right, Bishop, you think about it. But remember this:
Compatriots in glory!

BISHOP:

(*to the audience*) Quite a fellow.

The PIANO PLAYER performs a chord sequence,
then an announcement.

PIANO PLAYER:

The Dying of Albert Ball.

BISHOP recites a ballad in the style of
Robert Service.

BISHOP:

He was only eighteen
When he downed his first machine,
And any chance of living through this war was small;
He was nineteen when I met him,
And I never will forget him,
The pilot by the name of Albert Ball.

No matter what the odds,
He left his fate up to the gods,
Laughing as the bullets brushed his skin;
Like a medieval knight,
He would charge into the fight,
And trust that one more time his
   pluck would let him win.

O he courted the Reaper
Like the woman of his dreams,
And the Reaper smiled each time he came to call;
But the British like their heroes
Cold and dead, or so it seems,
And their hero in the sky was Albert Ball.

But long after the fight,
Way into the night,
Cold thoughts, as dark as night would fill his brain;
For bloodstains never fade,
And there are debts to be repaid,
For the souls of all those men who died in vain.

So when the night was dark and deep,
And the men lay fast asleep,
An eerie sound would filter through the night;
It was a violin,
A sound as soft as skin,
Someone was playing in the dim moonlight.

There he stood, dark and thin,
And on his violin
Played a song that spoke of loneliness and pain;
It mourned his victories,
It mourned dead enemies
And friends that he would never see again.

Yes, he courted the Reaper
Like the woman of his dreams,
And the Reaper smiled each time he came to call;
But the British like their heroes
Cold and dead, or so it seems,
And their hero in the sky was Albert Ball.

It's an ironic twist of fate
That brings a hero to the gate,
And Ball was no exception to the rule;
Fate puts out the spark
In a way as if to mark
The fine line between a hero and a fool.

Each time he crossed the line,
Albert Ball would check the time
By an old church clock reminding him of home;
The Hun came to know
The man who flew so low
On his way back to the aerodrome.

It was the sixth of May,
He'd done bloody well that day;
For the forty-fourth time, he'd won the game;
As he flew low to check the hour,
A hail of bullets from the tower –
And Albert Ball lay dying in the flames.

But through his clouded eyes
Maybe he realized,
This was the moment he'd been waiting for,
For the moment that he died
He was a hero, bona fide –
There are to be no living heroes in this war.

For when a country goes insane,
Obsessed with blood and pain,
Just to be alive is something of a sin;
A war's not satisfied
Until all the best have died –
And the Devil take the man who saves his skin.

But sometimes, late at night,
When the moon is cold and bright,
I sometimes think I hear that violin;
Death is waiting, just outside,
And my eyes are open wide,
As I lie and wait for morning to begin.

For I'm courting the Reaper
Like the woman of my dreams,
And the Reaper smiles each time I come to call;
But the British like their heroes
Cold and dead, or so it seems,
And my name will take the place of Albert Ball.

BISHOP and the PIANO PLAYER sing "Friends Ain't S'posed to Die."

BISHOP & PIANO PLAYER: (*singing*)
Look at the names on the statues,
Anywhere you go,
Someone was killed
A long time ago;
I remember the places,
I remember a time –
Those were the names of friends of mine.

The statues are old now
And they're fading fast,
Something big must have happened
Way in the past;
The names are so faded
You can hardly see –
The faces are always young to me.

Chorus

Friends ain't s'posed to die 'til they're old,
And friends ain't s'posed to die in pain;
No one should die alone when he is twenty-one,
And living shouldn't make you feel ashamed.

I can't believe how young we were back then.
One thing's for sure, we'll never be that young again.
We were daring young men, with hearts of gold.
And most of us never got old.

> *The song ends. Abruptly the PIANO PLAYER raps*
> *repeatedly on the piano as BISHOP assumes the*
> *character of CEDRIC the butler.*

CEDRIC:

Wakey, wakey, Bishop! Wakey, wakey! Rise and shine!

BISHOP:

(*drowsy and hungover*) Cedric? What's the idea, waking me up in the middle of the night.

CEDRIC:

It's bloody well eleven o'clock. And Madam has a bone to pick with you.

BISHOP:

All right, all right, I'll be right there.

> *He stands and faces the chair where, presumably,*
> *LADY ST. HELIER is seated.*

Good morning, Granny.

LADY ST. HELIER:

Bishop. Sit down. I have a bone to pick with you. Cedric, the colonial is under the weather. Bring tea and Epsom salts. (*to BISHOP*) Where were you last night?

BISHOP:

I was ... I was out.

LADY ST. HELIER:

Very good. Very specific. Well, I have my own sources, and the picture that was painted for me is not fit for public viewing: disgusting, unmannered, and informal practices, in company that is unworthy even of you. But what concerns me is not where you were, but where you were not – to wit, you were not at a party which I personally arranged, at which you were to meet Bonar Law, Chancellor of the Exchequer. What do you have to say in your defence?

BISHOP:

Now look, Granny –

LADY ST. HELIER:

I'll thank you not to call me Granny. The quaintness quite turns my stomach.

BISHOP:

Look, that was the fourth darn formal dinner this week – first it's General Haig, then what's-his-name, the parliamentary secretary ... I wanna have some fun!

A severe pause.

LADY ST. HELIER:

Bishop, I am only going to say this once: it is not for you to be interested, amused, or entertained. You are no longer a rather short colonial with poor taste and a bad service record. You are a figurehead. A dignitary. The people of Canada, England, the Empire, the world, look to you as a symbol of victory – and you will act the part. You will shine your shoes and press your trousers. You will refrain from spitting, swearing, public drunkenness – and I say this with emphasis: you will keep your appointments with your betters! Now tonight you are having dinner with Lord Beaverbrook, tomorrow with Attorney General F.E. Smith. Need I say more?

BISHOP:

No. No. I'll be there ... Granny.

LADY ST. HELIER:

Good. Oh, and Bishop, I had the occasion to pass the upstairs bathroom, and I took the liberty of inspecting your toilet kit. There is what I can only describe as moss growing on your hairbrush, and your after-shave smells like cat urine. I believe the implications are clear? (*to the PIANO PLAYER*) Cedric, a difficult road lies before us. Empire must rely for her defences on an assemblage of Canadians, Australians, and blacks. And now the Americans.

CEDRIC:

Oh no.

LADY ST. HELIER:

Exactly. Our way of life is in peril!

*The PIANO PLAYER plays a bouncy tune while
BISHOP, slightly drunk, composes a letter to
Margaret.*

BISHOP:

Dearest Margaret. I'm not sure I can get through this evening. In the next room is Princess Marie-Louise and four or five lords and ladies I can't even remember. I drank a little bit too much champagne at supper tonight and told the princess a lot of lies. Now I'm afraid to go back in there because I can't remember what the lies were, and I'm afraid I'll contradict myself and look like an idiot. Being rich, you've got a lot more class than me. They'd like you. Maybe we ought to get married. Thinking of you constantly, I remain ...

*The PIANO PLAYER begins to sing "Who Wants to
Go Back Home." BISHOP joins in.*

BISHOP & PIANO PLAYER: (*singing*)
   O when you steal a girl
   From an English Earl,
   Who wants to go back home?
   Just a Canadian boy,
   England's pride and joy,
   Who wants to go back home?
   You may be a king on English ground,
   But when you go back to your old hometown,
   They'll find ways to shoot you down –
   Who wants to go back home?

   O, baby, I'm so far from home,
   And I'm all alone,

And I'm saving England's ass,
And although I'm not your class,
I've got a chest that's full of brass –
Why don't you
Give me a kiss before I hit the sky,
One if I live, two if I die,
And maybe a third before we say goodbye –
Who wants to go back home?

> *BISHOP goes quiet as PIANO PLAYER sings*
> *final verse.*

PIANO PLAYER: (*singing*)
The prime of life,
The best of men,
It will never be like this again;
Who wants a life of remember when –
Who wants to go back home?
Who wants to go back home?

> *The song ends. Abruptly, the music takes on a*
> *more sinister quality. The following sequence is*
> *told and acted out to music in much the same*
> *way as the air battle scene in Act One, except*
> *the quality of the boy's adventure story is entirely*
> *gone now. What remains is adrenaline and fear*
> *and deadly concentration.*

BISHOP:
I woke up at three o'clock in the morning and, Jesus, was I
scared – very tense, you know? I mean, Albert Ball said
you couldn't do it with just one guy, and Albert Ball was a

maniac. But I figure it's no different than what we do every day, so what the hell. I mean, it's no worse. I don't think. Trouble is, nobody has ever attacked a German aerodrome single-handedly, so it's chancy – you know what I mean? I put my flying suit over my pyjamas, grab a cup of tea, and out I go. It's raining. Lousy weather for it, but what can you do? Walter Bourne, my mechanic, is the only other man up. He has the engine running and waiting for me.

He takes the part of BOURNE.

BOURNE:

Bloody stupid idea if you ask me, sir. I would put thumbs down on the whole thing and go back to bed if I was you, sir.

BISHOP:

Thanks a lot, Walter. That's really encouraging.

BOURNE:

It's pissing rain, sir. Bleeding pity to die in the pissing rain. I can see it all now, right before me very eyes. First, Albert Ball gets it. Then Captain Bishop gets it. I mean, it's a balls-up from beginning to end. Why don't you just take my advice and go back to bed like a good lad, sir?

BISHOP:

Why don't you shut up, Walter. Ready?

BOURNE:

Ready, sir!

The plane takes off to music.

BISHOP:

God, it's awful up here. Pale grey light, cold, lonely as hell. My stomach's bothering me. Nerves? Naw, forgot to eat breakfast, just one more thing to put up with. RRRrrr. I climb to just inside the clouds as I go over the line. No trouble? Good. Everybody is asleep. Let's find the German aerodrome. RRRrrr. Where is it? Should be right around here.

Musical sting as he spots something.

All right: a quick pass, a few bursts inside those sheds just to wake them up, then pick them off one by one as they try and come up. (*He starts the attack, then stops abruptly.*) Wait a minute! Wait a minute! There's no planes! There's no people – the bloody place is deserted! Well shit, that's that, isn't it? I mean, I can't shoot anyone if there's nobody there to shoot. Bloody stupid embarrassment, that's what it is. RRRrrr. Feeling really miserable now, I cruise around looking for some troops to shoot them. Nothing! What the hell's going on around here, is everyone on vacation?

Musical sting.

Suddenly I see the sheds of another German aerodrome, ahead and slightly to the left. Dandy. Trouble is, it's a little far behind the lines, and I'm not exactly sure where I am, but it's either that or go back. My stomach's really bothering me now – why didn't I eat breakfast? And why didn't I change out of my pyjamas? That's going to be great if I'm taken prisoner, real dignified – spend the rest of the war in my bloody pyjamas. RRRrrr. Over the aerodrome at about three hundred feet – Jesus, we've got lots of planes here, lots and lots of planes: six scouts – and a two-seater. Hope that two-seater doesn't come up for me. I'll have a hell of a time getting him from the rear. It's a little late to think about that now!

Engine noise and machine-gun fire from the
PIANO PLAYER.

AKAKAKAKAKAKAK! RRRRRrrrrr!

I don't know how many guys I got on that first pass, a lot of guys went down, a lot of guys stayed down. I shot up some of their planes pretty bad –

Gunfire from the PIANO PLAYER.

I forgot about the machine guns guarding the aerodrome! Bullets all around me, tearing up the canvas on my machine; just so long as they don't hit a wire. Keep dodging! Rrrr! Rrrr! I can't get too far away or I'll never pick them off as they try and come up – come on, you guys, come on! One of them's starting to taxi now. I come right down on the deck about fifteen feet behind him. AKAKAKAKAK! He gets about six feet off the ground, does this weird somersault, and smashes into the end of the field. I pull her around as quick as I can – RRRrrr – just in time to pick up another fellow as he tries to come up. AKAKAKAKAK! My tracers are going wide but the guy is so frightened he doesn't watch where he's going and smashes into some trees at the end of the field. I put a few rounds into him and pull back on the stick. RRRrrr! I'm feeling great now, I don't feel scared, I don't feel nothing, just ready to fight. Come on, you bastards, come on!

Musical sting.

Wait a minute, wait a minute. This is what Ball was worried about – two of them are taking off from opposite directions at the same time. Now I feel scared – what do I do now? Get the hell out, that's what you do!

Gunfire from the PIANO PLAYER.

One of them is close enough behind me to start firing. Where's the other one? Still on the ground. All right, you wanna fight? We'll fight! I put her into a tight turn, he stays right with me – but not quite tight enough. As he comes in for his second firing pass, I evade him with a lateral loop, rudder down off the top, and drop on his tail – AKAKAKAK! I hit the man. The plane goes down and crashes in flames on the field. Beautiful.

Gunfire from the PIANO PLAYER.

The second man is closing on me. I have just enough time to put on my last drum of ammunition. I fly straight at him, the old chicken game. I use up all my ammunition –

Both BISHOP and the PIANO PLAYER fire.

AKAKAKAKAKAK! I miss him, but he doesn't want to fight. Probably thinks I'm crazy. I've got to get out of here, they will have telephoned every aerodrome in the area, there will be hundreds of planes after me. I climb and head for home. RRRrrr.

The music becomes eerie.

All by myself again, at last. Am I going the right way? Jesus, my stomach! Sharp pains like I've been shot. (*feels his stomach and looks at his hand*) Nope, no blood. Good, I haven't been shot. It's just the excitement, on an empty stomach. Being frightened. Jeez, I think I'm going to pass out. Don't pass out, don't pass out ...

Silence on piano, followed by ominous punctuation.

Then I look up, and my heart just stops dead then and there. I'm not kidding. One thousand feet above me, six Albatros scouts. And me with no ammunition. I think I'm going to puke – don't puke, don't puke! Fly under them, maybe they won't see you. RRRrrr. I try to keep up. For a mile I fly under them, just trying to keep up. RRRrrr. I've got to get away. They're faster than me, and if they see me, they got me, but I've got to get away! I dive and head for the line ... (*sudden silence*) I can feel the bullets smashing into my back any second, into my arms, into my legs, into my ...

He looks up. A chord on piano.

Nothing. Jeez, they didn't see me. RRRrrr. Filescamp. Home. Just land it, take it easy. I land. Walter Bourne is there with a group of the others.

BOURNE:

I'm standing around, waiting for him to be phoned in missing, when there he comes. Like he's been sightseeing. He lands with his usual skill, cracking both wheels, then comes to a halt, just like usual – 'cept there's nothing left of his bloody machine. It's in pieces, bits of canvas flopping around like laundry in the breeze. Beats me how it stayed together. Captain Bishop sits there, quiet-like. Then he turns to me and he says, "Walter, I did it."

BISHOP:

(*completes the speech as himself*) I DID IT. Never had so much fun in my life!

A minor chord on the piano. It's not all triumph.

That was the best fight I ever had. Everybody made a very big deal of it – but I just kept fighting all summer, my score kept getting higher and higher, and I was feeling good. By the middle of August, I had forty-three – one less than Albert Ball. And that's when the generals and colonels started treating me funny.

Reprise of going-to-war music from Act One.
BISHOP plays himself and GENERAL TRENCHARD.

TRENCHARD:

Bishop! We have lots of medals for you, lots and lots of medals – and that's not all. You will receive your medals, you will go on extended Canada leave, and you won't fight again.

BISHOP:

Excuse me, sir, what did you say?

TRENCHARD:

Have I got a speech impediment, Bishop? I said you won't
fight again.

BISHOP:

Not fight again? I gotta fight again! I've got forty-three, Ball
had forty-four, all I need is one more of those sons of ...

TRENCHARD:

Bishop! You have done very well. You will receive the
Victoria Cross, the Distinguished Service Order, the Military
Cross. No English pilot has done that – not even Albert
Ball, God rest his soul. Leave it at that, Bishop. You have
done England a great service. Thank you very much. Now
you don't have to fight anymore. I should think you'd
be delighted.

BISHOP:

You don't understand, sir. I like it.

TRENCHARD:

Well, of course you like it. That is hardly the point. You see,
Bishop, you have become a colonial figurehead.

BISHOP:

I know, sir. A dignitary.

TRENCHARD:

A *colonial* dignitary, Bishop. There is a difference. You see,
Bishop, the problem with your colonial is that he has a
morbid enthusiasm for life. You might call it a *life wish*. Now

what happens when your colonial figurehead gets killed? I'll tell you what happens. Colonial morale plummets. Despair is in the air. Fatalism rears its ugly head. But a living colonial "hero" – that's a different cup of tea. The men are inspired. They say, "He did it and he lived. I can do it, too." Do you get the picture, Bishop?

BISHOP:

I believe I do, sir.

TRENCHARD:

Good lad. You shall leave Sixty Squadron, never to return, on the morning of August 17th. That is all.

BISHOP:

(*to the audience*) Well, that still gives me a week. A lot can be done in a week.

In the next six days, I shot down five planes. I really was Number One now. And the squadron, they gave me a big piss-up on my last night. But something happened in that last week that made me fairly glad to get out of it for a while. It was number forty-six.

Spoken to the "Lovely Hélène" waltz.

It's dusk. Around eight o'clock. I'm returning to Filescamp pretty leisurely because I figure this is my last bit of flying for a bit. It's a nice, clear evening, and when it's clear up there in the evening, it's very, very ... pretty. Suddenly, I see this German Aviatik two-seater heading right for me. It's a gift: I don't even have to think about this one. I put the plane down into a steep dive and come underneath him and just rake his belly with bullets. Well, I don't know how they built those machines, but the whole thing just fell apart before my very eyes. The wings came off, bits of the fuselage just collapsed ... and the pilot and the gunner, they fall free! Now I'm pretty sure I didn't hit them, so they are alive and there is nothing I can do to help them or shoot them or anything. All I can do is just sit there and watch those two men fall, wide awake ... to die. It's awful! I know I've killed lots of them, but this is different. I watch them falling, down, down, down, one minute, two minutes, three minutes ...

The music descends, gently.

It's like I can feel them looking at me.

The PIANO PLAYER hits a soft bass note. BISHOP takes a moment to recover.

So when I leave for London the next day, I'm pretty glad to be going after all.

The PIANO PLAYER plays part of "You're a Typical Canadian," indicating a return to London and LADY ST. HELIER.

LADY ST. HELIER:
Bishop, today you will meet the King. This represents a high-water mark for us all, and you must see to it that you do not make a balls-up of it. I understand the King is particularly excited today. It seems this is his first opportunity of presenting three medals to the same

gentleman. Furthermore, the King is amused that that gentleman is from the colonies. The King, therefore, may speak to you. Should you be so honoured, you will respond politely, in grammatically cogent sentences, with neither cloying sentimentality nor rude familiarity. You shall speak to the King with dignity and restraint. Do you think you can manage that, Bishop? Is it possible that the safest course would be for you to keep your mouth shut?

Again, a phrase from "You're a Typical Canadian"
on piano.

BISHOP:

I arrived at Buckingham Palace – late. It is very confusing.

ADJUTANT:

Excuse me, sir, but where do you think you're going?

BISHOP:

Oh. Um. I'm supposed to get a medal or something around here.

ADJUTANT:

Oh, you're way off, you are, sir. This is His Majesty's personal reception area. You just about stumbled into the royal loo!!!

OFFICER:

What seems to be the problem around here?

ADJUTANT:

(*to OFFICER*) Well, the colonial here wants a medal. But his sense of direction has failed him.

OFFICER:

Come along, Bishop, we've been looking all over for you. Now the procedure is this: ten paces to the centre, turn, bow ...

> *The PIANO PLAYER strikes up "Land of Hope and Glory."*

It's started already. Bishop, you're just going to have to wing it!

> *The music continues as a processional.*

BISHOP:

Here comes the King with his retinue, Order of St. Michael, Order of St. George, and here's me. The King pins three medals on my chest. Then he says ...

> *The PIANO PLAYER takes the part of KING GEORGE.*

KING GEORGE:

Well, Captain Bishop! You've been a busy bugger!

BISHOP:

(*to the audience*) I'm not kidding. The King is standing here and I'm standing here. The King speaks to me for fifteen minutes. I can't say a word. But after the investiture come the parties, the balls, the photographers, the newspaper reporters, the Lords and Ladies, the champagne, the filet mignon, and the fifty-year-old brandy. And here's me. Billy Bishop, from Owen Sound, Canada, and I know one thing –

this is my day! There will never be another day like it! I think of this as we dance far into the night, as we dance to the music of ... the Empire Soirée.

BISHOP & PIANO PLAYER: (*singing alternate lines, then singing together for the chorus*)

Civilizations come and go (don't you know),
Dancing on to oblivion (oblivion),
The birth and death of nations,
Of civilizations,
Can be viewed down the barrel of a gun.

Nobody knows who calls the tune,
It's been on the hit parade so many years,
You and I must join the chorus,
Like ancestors before us,
And like them ... we're going to disappear.

Chorus

You're all invited to the Empire Soirée,
We'll see each other there, just wait
    and see (wait and see);
Attendance is required at the Empire Soirée,
We'll all dance the dance of history.

Revolutions come and go (come and go),
New empires will take each other's
    place (take their place),
The song may be fun,
But a new dance has begun,
When someone points a gun at someone's face.

Alexander and Julius had their dance (had their chance),
'Til somebody said, "May I cut in?" (with a grin),
All you and I can do,
Is put on our dancing shoes,
And wait for the next one to begin.

Chorus

You're all invited to the Empire Soirée,
We'll see each other there, just wait
    and see (wait and see);
Attendance is required at the Empire Soirée,
We'll all dance the dance of history.

The song ends abruptly, followed by the opening
chords to "Off to Fight the Hun," and the PIANO
PLAYER sings.

PIANO PLAYER: (singing)
We were off to fight the foe,
We would change the world, although
How little had we travelled,
And how little did we know.

Now the young will fight the foe,
And we watch them as they go.
Somehow it doesn't seem like war
At all, at all, at all;
Somehow it didn't seem like war at all.

*At this point there are two alternate concluding
scenes, depending on whether the part is being
played by a young or an old man.*

FOR A YOUNG ACTOR

*BISHOP exits during the song to reappear as a
middle-aged man in a World War II uniform. He
faces the audience and gives a speech as though
to rally the troops.*

BISHOP:

I have seen you go, and my heart is very proud. Once
again, in the brief space of twenty years, our brave young
men rush to the defence of the Mother Country. Again you
must go forward, with all the courage and vigour of youth,
to wrest mankind from the grip of the Iron Cross and the
swastika. Once again, on the edge of destiny, you must test
your strength. I know you of old, I think. God speed you.
God speed you, the Army, on feet and on wheels, a member
of which I was for so many happy years of my life. God
speed you the Air Force, where, in the crucible of battle,
I grew from youth to manhood. God speed you and God
bless you. For, once again, the freedom of mankind rests in
you: in the courage, the skill, the strength, and the blood of
our indomitable youth.

*The speech ends on a grand note. Then BISHOP
stops and looks at the audience with a certain
amount of bewilderment. He speaks to the
audience as though to an old friend.*

You know, I pinned the wings on my own son this week. Margaret and I are very proud of him. And our daughter. Three Bishops in uniform, fighting in the same war. Well, I guess I'm on the sidelines cheering them on ...

FOR AN OLD ACTOR

> *The PIANO PLAYER segues from "Off to Fight the Hun" to a gentle reprise of the "Dearest Margaret" theme as BISHOP narrates a last letter.*

Dearest Margaret. I think when you haven't been in a war for a while, it comes as a bit of a surprise ... how much you miss it. That survival is really ... just a reprieve. And so you watch your children, and other people's children, go to war. And you're on the sidelines – cheering them on ... And now the faithful Lethbridge will put me to bed. I haven't felt this good in weeks. Thinking of you constantly, I remain ...

> *The ending of the play is the same, whether the actor playing BISHOP is young or old. The PIANO PLAYER plays a haunting, slightly discordant version of "In the Sky."*

BISHOP:

You know, it comes to me as a surprise that there is another war on. We didn't think there was going to be another war, back in 1918. Makes you wonder what it was all for. But then again, none of us are in control of these things, are we? And all in all I'd have to say ... it was a hell of a time.

BISHOP sings, a cappella.

O the bloody earth is littered
With the fighters and the quitters,
You can hear those soldiers yearning,
"O if only I could fly!"
In the burning sun I'll sight you,
In the burning sun I'll fight you –
O let us dance together in the sky.

BISHOP & PIANO PLAYER: (*singing quietly*)
  In the sky,
  In the sky,
  Just you and I up there together,
  Who knows why?
  One the hunter, one the hunted,
  A life to live, a death confronted,
  O let us dance together in the sky.

  The PIANO PLAYER plays a closing series
  of chords.

END

ACKNOWLEDGEMENTS

Though commonly billed as a "one-man show" and sometimes as a "two-man show," the evolution of *Billy Bishop Goes to War* has benefited from the creative contributions of many colleagues, listed here in more or less chronological order:

Paul Thompson
Lorna Gail Peterson
Paul Williams
Christopher Wootten
Renée Paris
Cedric Smith
Ross Douglas
Lewis Allen
Mike Nichols
Jennifer Tipton
David Gropman
Tommy Smith
Martin Bragg
Sue Lepage
Kevin Lamotte
Albert Schultz
Ted Dykstra
Camilla Koo
Barbara Willis-Sweete
Susan Maggi
Charlie Gray

JOHN MACLACHLAN GRAY

John MacLachlan Gray is a multiple award–winning writer and composer for stage, television, film, radio, and print.

Over the past four decades he has worked as a composer, librettist, and director of nine stage musicals; as a satirist on CBC-TV's *The Journal*; as a columnist for the *Globe and Mail* and the *Vancouver Sun*; as a screenwriter of feature films; and as the author of two works of non-fiction and five acclaimed novels.

He holds honorary doctorates from Mount Allison University and Dalhousie University, and is an officer of the Order of Canada.

Published Work

Novels	*Not Quite Dead* (2007)
	White Stone Day (2005)
	The Fiend in Human (2002)
	A Gift for the Little Master (2000)
	Dazzled: A Novel (1984)
Non-Fiction	*Lost in North America: The Imaginary Canadian in the American Dream* (1994)
	I Love Mom: An Irreverent History of the Tattoo (1994)
Plays	*Local Boy Makes Good: Three Musicals* (1987)
	Don Messer's Jubilee
	Eighteen Wheels
	Rock and Roll
	Billy Bishop Goes to War (1981)

ERIC PETERSON

Eric Peterson's career as a Canadian actor spans more than forty years.

He has performed leading roles on stages throughout Canada, on Broadway, in London's West End, at the Edinburgh International Festival, and at the Melbourne Festival.

In the mid-1970s, Peterson and Gray were members of Theatre Passe Muraille in Toronto, a company devoted to the creation of original Canadian theatre, which became the formative event of their early careers and inspired *Billy Bishop Goes to War*.

Peterson's credits in Canadian film and television include continuing roles as Leon Robinovitch on *Street Legal*, as Judge Malone on *This Is Wonderland*, and as Oscar Leroy on *Corner Gas*. He played featured roles in Jerry Ciccoritti's *Trudeau* and Deepa Mehta's *Earth*, as well as guest-star appearances on series such as *Slings and Arrows*, *Da Vinci's Inquest*, *Murdoch Mysteries*, *Dan for Mayor*, and *Republic of Doyle*.

In 2009, he received the Gordon Pinsent Award of Excellence for his theatre work, as well as the Canadian Gemini's Earle Grey Award – a lifetime achievement award for his film and television work. He holds an honorary doctorate from the University of Saskatchewan, and is a member of the Order of Canada.

Find out more about Eric Peterson's work in film and television on Internet Movie Database, www.imdb.com/name/nm0677139/